Never On A Sunday

Memories of the Stiperstones Mining Communities

Compiled by

Peter Francis
Jane Price
Kim Yapp

Editorial assistance

Tom Wall

Artwork

Jackie Astbury
Jilly Knill
Clifford Lewis
Malcolm Newton

Photography

Gordon Dickins

Published by

Scenesetters, Ash-Leys, Bucknell SY7 0AL
On behalf of the Shropshire Mines Trust

© Shropshire Mines Trust 2000

ISBN: 1 874200 10 6

SHROPSHIRE
MINES TRUST

A CHARITABLE TRUST

This project which began in January 1998 is especially dedicated to those who gave interviews, information and support but who are, sadly, no longer with us to have seen the project completed.

George Balmer
Gordon Cook
Emily Griffiths
Walton Humphrey
Malcom Newton
Nora Pinches
Jack Pugh

*"...they may rest from their labours;
for they take with them the record of their deeds"*
Revelation 14.13

Acknowledgements

This book could never have been brought to fruition without the help and support of very many individuals and organisations.

First we would like to thank most sincerely all those who allowed us to tape their memories. They provide the substance of the book. They are listed in alphabetical order in Appendix II.

We would further like to thank those who were interviewed or were able to give us specific information, including:
Gloria Rowson, Marcia Fletcher, Arthur Davies, Kate Gittins, Verna and Clifford Lewis, R Hulton-Harrop, Esmond Betton, Tom Gwilliam, Alan Buckley and the Reverend William Rowell.

For additional facts, practical help or sources of information our thanks are due to:-

Ken Lock for his support and interest and Johnny Butler, Clifford and Verna Lewis for all their assistance.

The Snailbeach and District Newsletter and The Minsterley Parish Magazine

The Mary Webb Society.

Peter and Julia Francis for the permission to use extracts from "Hasty Pudding and Kettle Broth", the diaries of the late Bill Francis.

The Evans family for the permission to use extracts from "Recalling the Past", recollections of the late George Evans.

Snailbeach Women's Institute.

All those who kindly let us borrow precious photographs.

The Community Council of Shropshire – we are especially grateful to Hilary Hymas for her encouragement and continued interest in this project.

The Shropshire Hills and Dales Project.

Awards for All – Millennium Lottery Fund.

'Back to Purple – conserving and restoring The Stiperstones': a Heritage Lottery Fund project run by a partnership of English Nature, Shropshire Wildlife Trust and Forest Enterprise with additional funding from the European Union and Tarmac.

English Nature.

John Powell for the production of archive material from the original tape recordings.

Landscape Radio and Recording.

Scenesetters for professional help and advice throughout this project and for publishing the book on behalf of the Shropshire Mines Trust.

Contents

In the beginning

South West Shropshire used to be famous for its lead mines. They lie in hill country dominated by the long rocky ridge of the Stiperstones, rising to 1760 feet above sea level. The lead mining area is small by comparison with others elsewhere in the country, yet in 1872 it produced over ten percent of the nation's lead ore.

Whilst this was an important lead mining area, the industrial activity never overwhelmed the landscape, most of which remained intensely rural. Indeed, the miners were often small-holders too. But the mines did sustain a higher population than would otherwise have been the case and a tightly-knit community developed. The themes of mining, farming and community recurred throughout the reminiscences from which this book is drawn and they give it a distinctive character and content. The mines closed long ago (the last in 1948) and today many fewer families are involved in farming, but the sense of community still exists.

Much has been researched and recorded about the mines along the Stiperstones, the technology used, the output of individual mines and the quality of the different ores. Some further information about the lead mining industry is contained in the appendix at the end of this book. Very little, however, has been written about the miners themselves and their families. They lived along the side of a wild, storm-battered hill range, immersed in superstition, dominated by religion and often living far away from their original birth place. Yet their churches and chapels are still there, surrounded by gravestones - some of them of relatively young miners and young children who fell victim to the virulent childhood diseases of that era, such as diphtheria, scarlet fever and tuberculosis.

The names of the hamlets and settlements along the Stiperstones ridge are unusual and the derivation of some of them uncertain. The name 'Snailbeach' leads to much discussion: whilst 'beach' almost certainly comes from the old word 'batch', meaning deep valley, the reason for the addition of 'snail' is anyone's guess. Whilst the picturesque names of Lordshill, Crowsnest, Mytton Dingle, Perkins Beach, Tankerville, The Red Ball, and Blakemoorgate conjure up pictures in a literary imagination, perhaps the reality was a little more stark.

Religion dominated the lives of the miners and their families. Sunday was a day of chapel services, Sunday school for the children and choir practices in the evening. Children could not play with a ball on a Sunday, sewing was forbidden and even the newspaper would be folded away on a Saturday night in favour of the Christian Herald. Hay would be left in the fields at risk of the elements and woe betide any housewife who hung washing out to dry! Hence the title of this book and the project which led to it: 'Never on a Sunday'.

Uncle Harry lived at Crowsnest and had a butcher's round; he had a shed where he cut up meat. He used to trade a bit with Tommy Griffiths from Minsterley and one Sunday morning Tommy came up and wanted to trade.
"How much do you want for that cow?" asked Tommy.
"No, I amma dealing today!" Uncle Harry replied.
"What d'you mean you amma dealing today?" he said.
"Well, it's Sunday", said Uncle Harry, "I dunna deal on a Sunday."
Tommy thought awhile.
"Well - if today was tomorrow how much would you want for it?"

Susie Hartshorn

The aim of the 'Never on a Sunday' project was to record interviews with as many as possible of the older residents of the Stiperstones area and those who had lived there in the past. More than sixty interviews took place. The people we spoke to were encouraged to tell their own story in their own words and to recall incidents and memories which were important to them. The taped interviews have been copied on to 'compact discs' which together will provide an archive of memories of rural life in the hill country of south west Shropshire. The discs will be available to those with an interest in the area and its past, and anyone wishing to make use of them should contact the Shropshire Mines Trust.

This book is a collection of extracts from those interviews. All we ask of the reader is that you enjoy and value them for what they are - individual recollections and individual perceptions. We have not set out here to write a history of the Stiperstones; rather our aim has been to record and reflect the precious memories that so many people have shared with us. Every effort has been made to research and confirm historical facts where they occur but, inevitably, some doubt and difference of opinion will remain. Please therefore accept these memories for what each one is - an individual's personal recollection of the past.

Memories, of course, have a historical context, though that context can sometimes be vague and unclear. Wherever appropriate therefore, we have tried to set quotes within their context by providing background information about the subject matter. As a broad guide, the majority of those we interviewed would have spent at least part of their childhood in the years between the two World Wars i.e. the 1920s and 1930s. A list of those interviewed and their dates of birth can be found in Appendix II. Where the War years

themselves are being referred to, we have endeavoured to make that clear - as we have with references to periods outside the above time scale. Memories passed on from parents and grandparents may, of course, relate to the later years of the 19th century.

Finally, when reading this book we would ask you to bear in mind the wise words of the late Bill Francis,

During the loneliness of old age one's thoughts revert to the days of one's childhood, remembering the good times forgetting the bad...... the lack of money, a penny was a fortune, the patched clothes, the darned socks and shoes with worn out soles. After all, one's neighbours were perhaps worse off. One forgets the midden in the yard and the smelly earth closet.

From "Hasty Pudding and Kettle Broth", the diaries of the late Bill Francis.

Ritton Castle Mine 1964.

1: All things bright and beautiful

The Stiperstones Church of England Primary School

When asked to recount their memories of years gone by, people move most easily to recollections of their childhood days. The years before the full burden of adult responsibility is assumed provide a rich source of stories spanning the full gamut of emotions. Idyllic and carefree they may not always have been, but memories of tears shed and hardships borne are sprinkled liberally with tales recalling laughter, mischief and fun.

Relationships within the extended family seem generally to have been close, and children looked no further for companionship and playmates than the community in which they spent their days. Many of those interviewed for this project have spent almost all their lives on or near the Stiperstones. Some at least of their childhood friends are often also living locally. Friendships have held firm and, even sixty or seventy years later, time can still be found for an occasional get-together and a happy chat about the shared days of childhood.

From the age of approximately five onwards, school began to assume a dominant role in most people's lives as it still does today. Children on the Stiperstones in the early years of the 20th century attended a number of different schools, depending principally on where they lived. These included: Minsterley, Stiperstones, The Bog, Shelve and Ratlinghope. Each one had its own method of working, standards of discipline and education. The daily journey to and from school was almost invariably on foot, in all weathers and sometimes over considerable distances. It was generally made in groups and provides almost as many remembered stories as does time spent in the playground and the classroom.

Although time for play and recreation was limited, and hardship and sometimes tragedy never far away, when childhood days spent on and around the Stiperstones are recalled, a quiet smile and a wry laugh are never far away.

Bath night, a necessary weekly ritual, involved a tin bath in front of an open fire. A clearly determined hierarchy of need established the order in which the bath water was used.

Bath night was hilarious, you'd start off with the youngest and keep on adding a drop more water to it 'til we'd all had a bath in front of the fire and then you'd got to carry it all out to the yard.

Millie Gough

Saturday night was bath night in front of the fire with the washing all around. We used to start on the cleanest first...... it was cosy though. Winter nights the extra bedding on my bed was father's army coat chucked across your feet, like.

Johnny Butler

A limited variety of sweets was available in the local shops. They were enjoyed sparingly.

Me mother used to buy a quarter of sweets a week, put 'em in a tin – boiled sweets or pear drops, sprinkle some sugar on and shake 'em up. We had one in a morning when we went to school or we could leave it 'til we came home at night and have it then.

Peggy Chidley

I can remember going to Jack Davies' shop and getting a farthing worth of licorice.

Derek Rowson

No, no we never used to bother with birthdays, didn't have cakes and presents then and we very rarely had sweets, very rarely. Well there weren't much money around then to buy sweets, again you bought your food.

Johnny Roberts

Johnny Roberts also remembers the daily tasks he was given responsibility for – and the consequences of not completing them.

Then we'd got so many jobs to do; there was morning sticks to get in to start the fire for the next morning, coal, there was getting hay in for the sheep and cows. Then you'd got to carry your water – about fifteen buckets of water, used to get it out of the little owd well down the side of the little owd lane in a yoke.
If them jobs wasn't done there'd be no tea for you, dad was very strict. If them jobs wasn't finished you were put to bed.

Johnny Roberts

Elsie Rowson's jobs included the fetching of milk from local farms. It was not a task she relished.

I fetched milk from Lower Hogstow, which I hated, Boat Level, and I didn't like that either, because by the time you got back to the road all the other children had gone on home so you had to go home on your own. I used to take a tin to school in a morning with a ha'penny in it, rattle it all the way to school – it was a wonder we didn't knock the bottom out! You'd hang it on your peg and I never once lost the money out of the can. It was always there.

Elsie Rowson

The boundary between Minsterley and Hope parishes went through the middle of the village of Snailbeach. As a result, some children walked each day across the fields to Minsterley school while others journeyed up the hill to the school at the Stiperstones. Children from the isolated hamlets and farmsteads at the southern end of the Stiperstones attended The Bog school, while Shelve school (actually some distance from the village of Shelve, on the A488 Shrewsbury to Bishops Castle road) served those living on the western slopes of the Stiperstones. In addition, children living 'over the other side' sometimes attended Ratlinghope school to the east on the lower slopes of the Long Mynd. The journey to school had to be made regardless of the weather.

Dad went whipping [working with the fox hounds] for Lord Harrop and we went to live over by the Gatten. We had to walk to Ratlinghope school, it was about four mile and four mile back again. You'd start out about half past seven in the morning and be there for nine and we'd walk back again at night. You had to go no matter what the weather was like – even if there was two foot of snow on the ground you had to go.

Johnny Roberts

Johnny Butler and Peggy Chidley were two of the Snailbeach children who travelled down to Minsterley for their schooling.

Mr Nixon was the school master at Minsterley, I can remember him breaking the cane on two lads.

Peggy Chidley

To go to school we went down the fields to Minsterley, joining up with the rest of the Snailbeach kids whose homes were in the Minsterley parish. If the fields were too wet then we all walked down the road, but then there were days when Mr Rowson's turn-out [pony and trap] would be going to Minsterley station with Nobby in the shafts. Nobby was a white pony who was loved by all. If there was room in the 'tub' then the kids from the farm rode in state. Then there came the day when Mr Rowson acquired a Model-T Ford car and with his son Clayton driving we were not denied a ride, nor in the lorry which was to follow. What wonderful memories of happy carefree days. If we fell out and fought it was soon over and done with but by and large we stuck together.

Johnny Butler

I had my hand rapped with a ruler for chatting. But it didn't do us any harm did it?

Eileen Higley

When we used to go to school across the fields to Minsterley old Mr Poole from the New House Farm would have it. They used to sow these small peas, you see, 'course he used to come to Minsterley school, his boots all undone, I can see him now – "Mr Nixon will you have a word with them Snailbeach kids? They'n bin in my pays [peas]!" Then another time he'd come, "Them Snailbeach kids 'as bin on agen – they'n bin in my swedes!" Course the boys used to carry a pocket knife with them and they'd peel one and share it out.

Peggy Chidley

The kids from Snailbeach used to come down to school through a field of beans and when they got there their pockets would be crammed with these beans.

It would be better walking to school down the fields than to go down the road it was so rutted and dusty. I took a bottle of tea in a stocking to school and left it in front of the fire to warm it up.

Jack Pugh

Elsie Rowson still remembers a kind act which brightened her very first day at the Stiperstones school.

We had a road-man, Matthew Price. I can see him now, a little red cheeked man, he wore oval gold rimmed glasses.

He was up on the road above Davies' farm when Leslie was taking me to school on my very first day and he gave me this lovely red apple, well I thought it was wonderful.

Elsie Rowson

There were three classes at the Stiperstones school, the infants, the middle room then the Headmaster's room. We used to do sums, history, geography, but I didn't like school very much and when I was fourteen I just left.

Ruth Chesters

I went to school with patches on me elbows but it didn't stop me learning, did it?

Mollie Rowson

We had slates and chalk at the Stiperstones school. My aunty who was Emily's mum (Emily Griffiths) and my mother taught here, but when they got married they had to leave.

Pupils and teachers of the Stiperstones School approx. 1920. From left to right. Back row: Miss Evans, Lallie James, Minnie Blakemore, Bertha Evans, Ethel Pugh, Miss Richard.
2nd row: Tom Rowson, Ivy Jane, Olive Vaughan, Rose Evans, unknown, Edith Pugh, Winnie Lewis, unknown.
Front row: George Bennett, Nellie Rowson, Nancy Lewis, Dolly Blakeman, Mary Corfield, Millie Pugh, Bill Evans.

We had to do compositions, sums and reading.

The headmaster, Mr Eastgate, lived in the school house. I suppose I was one of the older ones at twelve because he came to me one morning and said, "Will you keep the other children quiet because my wife had a baby in the night".

When it was school holidays we helped with the harvest and picked whinberries. We were never bored.

Margaret Buckley-Atkins

We moved here when I was five and a half (1938), from Devon. I hated school up here, I'd got a Devon twang and the kids called me names.

Mr Evans was the headmaster, Miss Jones was the junior teacher and Mrs Finn-Mason was the infant teacher and she was horrible. She had a long black dress on and an apron and a black hat. I remember I hated school when she was there. She made me draw a pear and my drawing was terrible and she'd got a cane and she'd tap your fingers. She wasn't very nice at all. Corfields were at the Vessons, they'd walk to school. I wouldn't go to school, I'd lie down or do anything and Betty Corfield would meet me and carry me to school. I didn't like it at all.

Betty Hordley

Even if it was really bad weather we would still walk to school, we would drag our desks up around the stove in the middle and we'd be allowed to draw. Perhaps we'd go home a bit early if it was really bad.

Susie Hartshorn

In his schooldays at the Stiperstones school, Graham France found that mischief and trouble were not things that he could easily avoid – and the consequences could be either painful or tedious.

When we were in class two I threw a conker at my sister Doreen. It landed on her lap and she didn't know where it was and it dropped to the floor. The headmaster said, "Stand up the boy that dropped that conker!" Of course Doreen had to stand up because SHE dropped it. He said, "I didn't expect that of you, you of all people!" She probably knew it was me, I think I chickened out there to be honest.

I had to stay in at the playtimes. I had to write the 119th Psalm I don't know how many times, it's the longest psalm of the lot. You had little pens you dipped in the inkwell. I'd *just finished doing it and it had taken a lot of playtimes. There was a big map on the wall so I got the pen and threw it and it landed in the map and it stuck in! Mr Evans walked in and caught me doing it, so I had to write the 119th Psalm again in playtimes.*

I probably had as many canings as anybody. Mr Evans used to give the cane four times on each hand. You daren't go home and tell your mum and dad or you'd get it again!

At the end of term the naughtiest boys got the job of washing the inkwells. Bill Evans and I used to have to wash all the inkwells and we got fed up with it. There was a holly bush the other side of the school yard so we threw them all in there! When they came back to school to put the inkwells in the proper little trays there were no inkwells to put in the trays! Bill and I were for it! I had to go out in the school yard and wear placards on me, "I MUST NOT FIDGET", "I MUST NOT......do this or that!"

Graham France

Mr Banks was a temporary teacher at the 'Beach' School (Stiperstones) and he used to call our Graham 'Mike and Herbert' because he was never still and always in mischief.

Doreen Rowson

In the days before school canteens provided a meal service of their own, a mid-day snack was either something you took with you each day or your mother brought along especially.

Sometimes on a Monday morning, perhaps, or during the week, we hadn't got enough bread and we'd go to school and at dinner time we would walk down to the quarry at the top of Paddock Bank and when we got down there mum had made a bit of stew and brought it up in the big milk tin. Oh, it would surely hold about half a gallon, this milk tin and she used to bring the dishes and spoons. I always remember sitting at the top of the quarry there having this stew for dinner.

Nellie Rowson

Stew would also be a mid-day meal for some children at The Bog school.

Instead of cutting sandwiches for the other three, mum used to make a big stew while they were up in school for the morning, and me and mum would go and meet them on

the road and sit down where the Black Pit was, and we'd sit on the side of the road there and of course I had to have a spoon as well, and we would eat out of this big bowl. We all used to tuck in.

Millie Gough

In relative terms, conditions at The Bog school seem to have been quite salubrious. Effective use was made of the advantages provided by the nearby mining activities.

We were all very well off at The Bog school, we were sort of spoiled. We had radiators, central heating, flushed toilets and hot water when nobody else around had got such modern facilities. That's because we had the water from the mines, it was piped down from there.

The children who lived on farms or small holdings and had got cows would bring a bottle of milk to school every morning and the elder girls would go out and make a large pan of cocoa for everybody about eleven o'clock with the milk that they brought. Nobody got paid for it.

The teachers were Miss Moss and Mrs Edwards. Miss Moss would take football and woodwork with the boys. They had to be very adaptable dealing with boys up to fourteen.

Millie Gough

Infants class at the Bog School. 1938. (from left to right) Back: Harvey Potter, George Groves, Cecil Jones, Mrs Jack Edwards, Joyce Munslow.
2nd row: Rosemary Downes, Doreen Swain, Joe Hotchkiss, Roy Munslow.
3rd row: Elsie Beddoes, Doreen Munslow, Olwyn Swain, Eileen Richards. Front: Brenda Hotchkiss, Sybil Evans.

I went to The Bog school, that was my college. There was a hundred and six children at one time aged between five and fourteen.

Henry Owen

Brenda Jones also has fond memories of her school days at The Bog.

I went to The Bog school. There was fifty of us with just two teachers. I loved maths, mental arithmetic I liked, I was really good at it, and spellings. But the trouble was my brother Joe, who was two and a half years younger, when he moved up into my class – I used to ask for spellings but I couldn't ask when he came up 'cos he was a real duffer at spellings.

We did a lot of needle work, tray cloths and runners where you ironed the pattern on and did cross stitch and stem stitch.

You never went to school in a uniform or your best clothes. You had hand downs, but they were clean.

Brenda Jones

John Francis spent much of his childhood on a small holding at the Grit. He had only a relatively short distance to travel each day to the nearby Shelve school.

We moved to Apple Tree Farm and I started school in the December at Shelve. We had two lady teachers, Mrs Ingram and Miss Purslow who came up on the milk lorry. We did history and geography and played football at lunchtime. Joe and Lou Evans were twins and they chose the teams. You never had a position. The lady teachers didn't understand football at all. If you could get a hundred Oxo coupons you could send away for a football. Sometimes we used a tennis ball.

John Francis

Mum always had a birch

Sometimes it seems that a rural childhood presents almost endless opportunities for mischief making and adventure. It is often such scrapes and tricks which live longest in the memory. Graham France was certainly involved in his fair share.

Mr Parry had Central Stores in Snailbeach. He had a Ford van with a canvas top for grocery deliveries. It was getting near to firework night and I had some sparklers, I lit one and threw it up in the air and it fell on the van and burnt the top clean off. Of course he had to go and see me father, I wasn't allowed out for a month or six weeks.

In the pub they had target shooting down the passage, when they had finished Walton [Humphrey] and I picked the rifle up and I pulled the trigger and shot a hole right through the window. It was lucky I didn't shoot Walton!

Old Mr Perkins had a house down in the hollow and he always had a stick and coal fire so we used to get a clod and a slate and put it on top of the chimney and it wouldn't half smoke him out!

When we were about ten years old we used to smoke. Walton used to get the cigarettes – I don't suppose we paid for them. Then we would go with Mr Humphrey, Walton's father, to Batchcott Hall [near Pulverbatch] for the day. We would be left to amuse ourselves, there was an old threshing machine in the yard with a chimney on it. Walton and I had got to hide the matches, we'd had a smoke and we were sat on this thing and decided to hide the matches down the chimney. Well it all went off with a whoosh 'cos there was fuel in it!

Graham France

Fireworks also provided an avenue for mischief for Mollie Rowson and her sister Nellie.

I remember me and Nellie putting a jackie jumper through somebody's door! And when the old folks left their washing out on the line we would get hay and stuff the washing, stuff the coms [combinations – undergarments] and that 'til they were full of hay.

Mollie Rowson

Hats were an almost obligatory element of outdoor clothing at one time. This was particularly so on a Sunday when black bowler hats were a very common sight among the menfolk. They were of course removed in chapel and the difficulty then was determining whose was whose!

Some bowler hats would have little pin holes in the crown and a person would know whose hat was whose by the pattern of the pinholes. There used to be a space at the back of the chapel and a shelf. Each and every one used to lay their bowler hats on there. Most gentlemen farmers had one. What we would do – we would get pins and poke them through the pinholes! And then when he'd put his hat on he'd wonder what had happened! Also we would swap them so they wouldn't know whose was whose! They'd be talking outside the chapel afterwards we would stand back and watch 'cos we'd be waiting there for our parents to go home. They would disappear carrying the wrong hat so it wouldn't be 'til they got home they found out they hadn't got the right hat!

Graham France

Mischief making, however, did not go unheeded or unchecked.

We used to have the birch. Mum always had a birch, a proper birch stick, plaited. I was terrible for laughing. If anybody started me laughing that was it. I'd have to go out in the wash house and had to stop there until the meal was finished.

Peggy Chidley

I often look back and think my dad must have thought that the way to bring up the perfect child was to thrape the hell out of him because I do not think a day passed without a damned good hiding!

From "Recalling the Past" by George Evans

As children we made our own pleasure

In small villages like those on the Stiperstones, children made use of the natural and man-made facilities around them to fashion their own play areas. In Snailbeach, the vast waste tips from the lead mines (known locally as the 'White Hillocks') provided an ideal ready-made playground.

You could let your children go, today you're scared to leave your children out of your sight, but you could let them go because they were safe. They played around the hillocks, we used to play Fox and Hounds, some would be foxes and go and some would be hounds and chase after them.

Sarah Ann Evans

We would play Hares and Hounds on a moonlit night, we'd climb up the old trestles on the aerial rope way. We've even

played football up by the Devil's Chair in the moonlight with snow on the ground.

Wallace Evans

We played skipping, hopscotch and rounders. We had great fun out of playing those games. We used to go over and play on the mine or the white hillocks. The lads played cricket or football on there and we made slides on the white slopes.

Ruth Chesters

The white hillocks and Halvans Engine House, Snailbeach

They'd get wood, planks of wood, and sit up on top of the white tip and down they'd come to the bottom. Poor old Fred Jones – there was a performance – he was "aaahing" and "oohing" and if I never tell a lie he had a splinter as long as THIS in his bottom! We had to take Fred to the local nurse that lived in the village. Never made no difference, after a bit Fred was on the plank again!

Peggy Chidley

I remember playing on the spar at the back before I started school – making mud pies decorating 'em with flower petals and leaves and trying to make sandcastles, but it wouldn't stick together, it used to run.

Elsie Rowson

We'd play bowlers – with an old bike wheel and a piece of stick and we'd play tops, some lads were experts throwing the tops and they'd land spinning and they'd whip them to keep them going. You were lucky to have a football at all, the older lads would come down from Pennerley to play with the local lads outside the school. They'd play with an old rag ball which was an old stocking stuffed with rags.

Bill Evans

We'd make little playhouses, bits of china and dock leaves – we'd do lots of pretending.

Susie Hartshorn

For Ruth Chesters, the narrow gauge Snailbeach District Railway will be forever linked with the fun and thrills of childhood.

The greatest thing happened coming home from the Stiperstones school. We would run all the way to see if we could get to the end of the railway line to have a ride on the engine coming across the back to the engine shed. Those were very happy days.

Ruth Chesters

For some local children the farm they lived on, or near, provided a more than adequate arena for games of skill, imagination and, sometimes, no small element of risk.

The farm was our playground and whatever Don Rowson dared you to do, you did. There was an iron rod across the width of the wainhouse [farm machinery shed], tying the walls in. He'd get us younger ones hanging on it to see who could hold on the longest and we'd be blue in the face before we'd be the first to let go. If he wanted you to hold his ferret, you held it! He had an airgun and I was the twit who held his cap out at arm's length for him to shoot at. He had a greyhound dog called Mick, he used to come around our house and run off with mother's porridge saucepan. With him, you knew where all the birds' nests were. He was an expert with a catapult. With a little bush covered in bird lime you went catching Sheriffs (goldfinches). With snow on the ground you propped a riddle up with a stick, with string attached and, hiding in the barn you waited until the birds came to feed on the bait and then pulled the string. One of the school managers at Minsterley school once lectured us on the evils of poaching.

Johnny Butler

We'd have little playhouses, Johnny Butler and me. We used to go to the place where mother threw all the broken crockery and go and get the nice pieces and make crockery for the playhouse. At the wainhouse at the farm there was clay underneath it and we used to get this clay and make marbles and take them in the house and put them in the oven to get hard. We'd make fruit and baskets out of the clay. We'd spend hours there. There was a swing in the wainhouse with a piece of wood for the seat, the rope had burnt the beam.

Della Pugh

With a little imagination, household furniture could be transformed into an adult world of adventure. Similarly, simple games – some virtually unheard of today – would provide hours of amusement for young minds.

A thing I used to do as a child, me dad had a Windsor armchair and I used to get some chairs in front of them and tie some cord to them and pretend they were the horses and I'd sit on the arms of the chair and pretend I was in the cart. I'd got a horse and cart and I'd be driving these horses.

Nellie Rowson

As children we made our own pleasure, we made bows and arrows, kites, tin whistles, spinning tops and whips.

Emily Griffiths

We played a game called Tip-Cat. The game was played with two pieces of stick. One, some four to six inches long, tapered at each end, was pitched into a circle. The nearest to centre went first, hitting it on the tapered end to cause it to spin up into the air, with the second length of stick some three foot long. While the short length was still in the air you hit at it. Each took his turn and the winner was the one who hit it the furthest. I was lucky if I hit it at all, I was the one with the glasses.

Johnny Butler

If you wanted a ball you made your own, a black stocking with some hay in the toe and then turned over and over and over will make a ball.

Della Pugh

We never used to go out much, we'd have to be in bed for seven o'clock. There'd be a gang of us go round together, expect I'd be about nine or ten years old. We used to do boxing of a night with candles on the wall.

It was a hard life and we used to make all our own fun.

Johnny Roberts

Children have always played with dolls and continue to do so today. The degree of sophistication has changed over the years, but endless delight and pleasure could always be obtained from even the most basic home made substitute.

I had a row of logs on the sofa and a stick and I was a school teacher and taught this row of logs. There wasn't the money for dolls.

Dolly Harrison

The only doll I ever had was from my Aunty Ruth and what we had for Christmas was what she sent in a parcel. Mum had got no money and dad had died when I was six, and we always used to look for this parcel coming at Christmas. One year it come and there was a doll in it and our Jessie went to look for the postman and he got the parcel and it was one of those dolls that would cry and he was tipping this owd parcel up and the doll was crying.

Mary Challinor

We'd sew them on mother's old machine. We'd make a body, turn them inside out and stuff 'em and then draw them a face and get some wool for their hair and make curls and plaits with a darning needle. We were taught to sew as girls from very young. We were taught to knit as well very young.

Della Pugh

I used to sit with Mr Fred Jones who was the local carpenter and undertaker and wheelwright. He used to make me curls with shavings from the brace-and-bit that he bored holes with. He used to say, "I'll make you some curls, my wench", and he used to get a piece of binder twine and put all these shavings around to make me some curls. I used to sit for hours with him in the carpenter's shop at the farm.

Della Pugh

SHAVINGS FOR CURLS

Christmas was the highlight of the year for youngsters on the Stiperstones, as it was (and still is) for children right across the globe. It was eagerly anticipated for months beforehand, and long remembered when it was all over. The traditional pleasures of Christmas, which people remember from the 1920s, '30s and '40s still remain the same today – carol singing, crackers, and of course, the visit of Father Christmas.

We'd go carol singing in little gangs, and the thing was to get in front of others that was singing and by the time you'd run to the next place you'd got no wind to sing – so you missed a verse out! We'd go around the village but it lasted a week not just Christmas Eve. By the time you'd finished you'd be up above Pennerley or at The Bog. Perhaps you'd be given a penny or tuppence to share between you, or an orange, and you'd walk all the way back then. At the end of it all you'd reckon it up, and if you'd got a couple or three bob it would keep you in shoe leather.

Johnny Butler

My christmas tree was a holly branch. On boxing day we all came down to The Farm to granny and grandad and you couldn't go in until you'd sung a carol at the door. Usually Mr and Mrs Harrison would come in with their family and we'd go into the big room and we'd all have a sing song.

Betty Hordley

I remember the last Christmas as I had me stocking filled. Mrs Cook took mam to town and I had a small sewing box. We'd have an apple and an orange and a few nuts in our stocking and I had this sewing box in mine. But I'd followed mam down the stairs very quietly, and there her was by the fire sticking these things, and I spoke, I tell you what, I never got no more, that was the end of Christmas stockings for me.

Dolly Harrison

At Christmas we had a few nuts in the toe of our stocking, perhaps an orange and an apple, a sweet mouse and a cracker.

Peggy Chidley

We didn't have many presents in those days. We used to have stockings of course with an orange and perhaps a half crown in the toe. You made your own dolls, a rag doll. We had two Staffordshire dogs which we took to bed, one was Meg and one was Bess. Mine was Meg, took 'em to bed for years. They were china.

Della Pugh

It was very rare we had any presents for Christmas – might have a sugar mouse, that's about all and a cracker, perhaps, with a little owd camel or a mouse in it. Birthdays were out of the question – I had nothing for me birthday nor me sister – used to forget them. You'd got no money to buy things then. 'Tinna like it is today – you got no value of it today!

Heber Rowson

For George Balmer, the memory of discovering Father Christmas remained vivid.

We were waiting up one night 'cos I said, "It seems funny Father Christmas bringing these stockings". About twelve o'clock the door opened, it was my sister Eva with the presents to fill the stockings. They used to put them on the settee downstairs when they were filled. What we got in the toe – it was always a sweet mouse, a white one with pink eyes. Always stuck right in the toe that was. Then there'd be oranges or apples.

George Balmer

As with all recollections of childhood, people tend to remember the happiest days. But some childhoods were marred by circumstance.

On the Stiperstones, the spectre of mining related illness could cast a long shadow. Johnny Butler recalls, as do many others, the effect it had on his father even when Johnny was still a young boy.

I never had a dad to play with if you understand, he hadn't got the breath to walk about.

Johnny Butler

I first went into hospital when I was about five years old. I was a cripple, I could only 'scrawl' about and I couldn't walk upright. I went to Oswestry Orthopaedic Hospital where I was in a men's ward with the soldiers. It was 1945 and there was no room in the children's ward. The soldiers had war wounds, they were fitted with artificial legs and that. There was a lot of amputations and disabilities. The ward was all open, the rain used to blow in on you, in the winter as well. I had plaster from me toes right up to me chest and I lay on me back for months. I was in six months the first time and six to seven months the second time. You didn't get visitors very often, once a fortnight, they'd have to come on the train. They would have walked to Minsterley Station to get to Shrewsbury. They could only stay for the time between trains. It was horrible, you didn't like it when they went. I would cry. But I could walk after. We had lessons in hospital even when I was in plaster. The teacher would come for an hour a day. For therapy you had to climb ladders up the wall and do exercises.

Doug Boulter

For some, childhood meant responsibility from a very early age.

My great grandmother died in childbirth and they carried her to Hope. My grandmother was only eleven and she had to look after the other two or three children, the youngest being only two. Her father was blind, he was blinded in the mines when he was thirty, dynamiting. They wanna very fussy in the mines in them days. His name was Arthur Rowson and they called him 'Blind Arthur'.

Tom Pinches

My mam was born up the Crowsnest Dingle, as was Bob and me. Mam went blind in her teens. Mam went away to live in Birmingham because my father went to work there. He was a journeyman, that means he was a blacksmith that did not hold his own business. He worked for another man. The First World War broke out on the 1st August 1914 and off he went and enlisted. Grandad Blakeman was a big soldier in the Boer War and so my dad volunteered. He had to bring mam home to his mother in Minsterley because she couldn't live on her own or go out without a guide. So she came to Minsterley with one little girl but there was summat the matter with her, she was a mongol or spina bifida or something and mum was expecting another baby. A month before she had us her mother-in-law died so she had to come back to her mam up the Dingle to stop with them 'til father came home, but he never came back.

When I was about two my aunty and mam's brother had a baby and it was born dead and her was very, very upset so he come up from Stockport to see if mam would let one of us go to 'em for a bit. Granny and grandad and mam had a bit of a conference and it was decided that the boy would be best to go. I'd be better looking after me mam. So he went and although we were twins we were never reared together. When he used to come on holiday I'd knock him about 'cos he was from the town; he wouldn't be there long afore I'd give him a clout and he'd say, "If you weren't a girl I'd hit you."

I used to take poor old mam to town when I was about six or seven and we'd walk to Minsterley to catch the train. There was no traffic but mam always took a duster in her pocket to polish our shoes on the train. We'd go in the shops, her'd say, "We want Maddox [department store in Shrewsbury], spell it out to me". I could see it and spell it so we'd go in there and there'd be somebody at once would come and say, "What counter do you want madam?" They'd take her and put her to sit down.

It was my job to get the water before I went to school or work, to get mam enough water for the day 'cos she couldn't get down the steps to get it.

I used to have a new frock, Mrs Parry from the shop was very good to me mam. She used to come up to see her just before the anniversary. "Mrs Blakeman" she'd say, "I'm going to Birmingham do you want a new dress for Dolly for the anniversary?" Mrs Parry used to choose it .

We were very, very happy but very, very poor.

Dolly Harrison

Doug Boulter remembers Dolly Harrison's mother,

A treat would be a packet of sweets, toffees perhaps. Dolly Harrison's mother used to make toffees and you'd have them in a cone. She'd sell them from home.

During the interviews carried out for Never on a Sunday one of the saddest memories, shared by many, was the plight of the two brothers Dennis and Terence O'Neill, at Bank Farm in the Hope Valley.

Dennis and Terence O'Neill were the sons of John Thomas O'Neill and Mabel Blodwyn O'Neill who lived in Newport, Gwent. Unable to cope with their eight sons, the authorities, in the form of the Newport Education Committee, arranged for three of the sons to be fostered. At the outset an official from the Education Committee had visited Bank Farm, stating in his report that it was clean and tidy and he was "favourably impressed" with Mr and Mrs Gough. He was of the opinion that the boy Dennis would be going to a good home where he would be well brought up.

Dennis, then aged twelve, duly arrived at the farm of Reginald and Esther Gough in the Hope Valley in June 1944. It was a farm of some seventy acres, and the Goughs made a living from cattle, pigs, sheep and poultry, without employing any outside help. Terence, aged nine, arrived soon after.

The Gough's matrimonial relationship appeared to be somewhat stormy, and Terence O'Neill, when questioned at the trial of Reginald Gough, confirmed that they had witnessed the couple fighting and swearing. Mrs Gough was forbidden by her husband to kiss the boys, and had quietly requested Terence not to kiss her in front of Mr Gough.

Within seven months Dennis O'Neill was dead. At the inquest the report of the pathologist Dr A J Rhodes of the Royal Salop Infirmary said that, "The body was thin and wasted, with wasted muscles and very little fat was found in the normal sites". He found no natural cause for the boy's death. The boy was definitely undernourished. He had a number of septic ulcers on his feet and severely chapped legs. However it was not the malnutrition and chronic sepsis that had killed Dennis but "Acute cardiac failure following violence applied to the front of the chest. Violence applied to the back by beating acted as a contributory factor".

The boys attended the Hope Church of England School where by November 1944 Dennis' attendance record had given cause for concern. No attendance was recorded for December but Mrs Gough had informed the school that both boys had chilblains and could not get their boots on. A routine visit by a member of the Newport Education Committee on December 20th 1944 raised concerns about Dennis' general appearance, advising Mrs Gough that he should perhaps see a doctor. A report was submitted to the Committee that there were misgivings about Dennis O'Neill, although both boys had said that they were perfectly happy.

Evidence was produced at the trial that Mrs Gough had written to the Newport Education Committee stating that she did not wish Dennis to stay at the farm when he reached school leaving age as he would be no use to them on the farm, he was incapable of washing himself and was dishonest, "This we are doing our best to correct". However, they would like to keep Terence who was stronger than Dennis and looked like being more useful on the farm. In his defence, Mr Gough catalogued misdemeanours committed by the boys for which he found it necessary to administer punishments. The boys were alleged to have been cruel to the chickens and calves at the farm, but Terence disputed the allegations in court.

A strict regime of punishment was enforced by the Goughs upon the two boys. Terence described 'stripes'. They would have ten stripes for one wrong; they were given on the hand with a stick. When they went to bed they had to count how many stripes they had to have for that day, and Mr or Mrs Gough would give them. Sometimes they would have one hundred stripes in one day. Terence went on to describe how Mr Gough tied Dennis naked to a pig bench and thrashed him with a stick until he cried. Dennis' crime had been to bite a bit out of a swede.

Being shut in a cubby hole was another form of punishment, as was being deprived of meals. Terence described Mrs Gough ordering him to get some bracken from the spinney but because it was covered in snow it was an impossible task and Terence was therefore not allowed any tea. Dennis was made to stand and watch the others eat at meal times as a form of punishment. Terence described their meagre diet, and the barrister for the prosecution described an incident wherein Dennis had got under the cows in order to suck their udders to get milk.

They had to wash in the yard in a bath. Dennis had to strip and hang his clothes on the pump outside. Terence could only remember one occasion when Mrs Gough bathed them with warm water, but even then she used a scrubbing brush.

Christmas 1944 arrived and the boys were given a

A view from the Stiperstones towards the Hope Valley

selection of presents which included books and games which Mrs Gough would play with them in the evenings.

But by January 8th 1945 Dennis, in extreme pain due to the condition of his feet, had his crying met with a severe thumping by Mr Gough. Next morning he suffered a fit after which Mrs Gough sent for the doctor. Dennis was dead before the doctor ever reached the isolated farm.

The conclusion of this sad tale was reported in The Wellington Journal, March 24th 1945:-

In the hushed Stafford Assize court the curtain was drawn on the Gough trial when Reginald Gough (31) of Bank Farm, Hope Valley, Minsterley, was found guilty of the manslaughter of Dennis O'Neill, who died on January 9th this year, and Gough's wife Esther, aged 29, was found not guilty of manslaughter but guilty of wilful neglect, Mr Justice Wrottesley having previously told the jury that there was no evidence against her of manslaughter.

Sentencing Gough to six years penal servitude the judge remarked, "You have shown a beastly cruelty and you killed partly by slow means and partly by swift means a boy whom you knew to be in your power. Whether you suffer from some terrible form of jealousy or not I do not know but your behaviour has, I think, rightly shocked the world and shocked England."

Gough was immediately escorted from the dock. Turning to Gough's wife Mr Justice Wrottesley had these words to say, "Yours is a very different case. It was hard perhaps to be tied to such a man and in charge of such children but your upbringing told you what your duty was and you did not do it. Nobody I think can but agree with the jury in what they have said. But I take into account the physical strain you have been under, your ill health and the fact you have been in prison already for a considerable period you will go to prison for six months."

2: Give us this day our daily bread

Food found its way onto the tables of Stiperstones families in the early years of the 20th century from a variety of sources. Few homes were without their own gardens from which much hard work could produce an impressive array of vegetables and other foods. Chickens were a familiar sight, producing a ready supply of fresh eggs and, when their best days were past, meat as well. It was the family pig, however, which evoked the most vivid and often fond memories.

People would also 'harvest' the fruits of the countryside which surrounded them. Whinberries (bilberries), cranberries (cowberries), blackberries and others were gathered, partly to supplement the family diet and partly because they could be sold to provide a timely injection of cash when, for example, a new pair of shoes or an outfit for school was needed.

Nuts were gathered and rabbits shot. In pre-myxomatosis days there was no shortage of rabbits on the slopes of the local hills and they provided a regular and staple element of family meals. The hamlets of the Stiperstones did boast a number of small shops and their services were supplemented by travelling salesmen coming up from places like Pontesbury. Purchases, however, were often restricted to items such as tea, sugar and salt – necessities which were not readily available elsewhere.

There were, of course, those for whom life was a constant struggle for survival, but for the most part Stiperstones people remember a regular meal on the table. It was a meal, nevertheless, which adults and children alike had to work to provide – and it was relished and appreciated all the more as a result.

A miner's cottage usually consisted of two rooms upstairs and one or two rooms downstairs with a pantry under the stairs. Sometimes a back kitchen would be added with a pent roof, and this usually contained a built-in washing boiler and in early days a baker's oven. The living room had a cast iron grate with a side oven and occasionally a boiler on the opposite side. This was the only cooking facility. A crane with hooks would dangle over the fire and from this would be suspended either a cast iron kettle, a cast iron frying pan or a three legged gypsy pot as required. The latter was used for boiling and stewing, often containing not only the meat course, usually rabbit, but also a suet dumpling tied up in a cloth. Fortunate people had a Dutch oven which clipped to the front bars of the grate.

Emily Griffiths

![A typical miner's home]

A typical miner's home

In comparison farmhouse kitchens had to cater for the needs of the family and the workforce.

A farm kitchen was always big and there was always an enormous table. The farms would feed the threshing gang and there would be nine of us and we would all sit down together. The first farm I went to I sat there and looked around and on the hearth there was a potato pan about two feet across. I had a dinner put before me I could hide behind, but I ate it. There was always loads of good wholesome food.

Connie Read

If you was lugging hay you'd got a field full of help, they never wanted any pay – they used to come in for supper, mother used to get the ham down and cook it with eggs and there'd be pickles and they would enjoy it. You could almost have a meal with the smell.

Wallace Evans

Food and water had to be stored and preserved as effectively as possible:

There was a porch over the door with a seat across and we'd put two buckets of water there and cover them over with wood covers that dad made. You filled your kettle from there.

Millie Gough

In our pantry we always kept a stein [large earthenware vessel] of water, clean water, it was carried the day before. There were no fridges, there was no greaseproof or that kind of thing in those days. You covered any food up with a basin or as best you could. You just had your pantry shelves. Almost always there was a bench in the pantry. You had to buy your food as you went on, our mum had to pay for one lot on a Wednesday for what we ate the week before and we'd start again then.

Mollie Rowson

Marcia Addy. All water had to be carried.

We had all our water from Peggy's Well in the Crowsnest Dingle, it used to be bricked around. It was not very deep and the water was continually bubbling up. It was really beautiful water.

Derek Rowson

The cottagers would give a hand to plant and harvest the potatoes and have a row or two for themselves when they got the potatoes up. We children used to pick them up. We would have three buckets; one for small ones for the pigs, one for next year's seed and the other for eating. My father used to store them in tumps. He would dig a nice round hole about nine inches deep and three feet across. He would then go on the hill to where the whinberry wires grew and with a spade, he would cut a sod about two feet wide and three feet long which he rolled up from the ground like a carpet. He would then cover the potatoes in the tump with the sod, whinberry wires down against the potatoes. Then he would cover it all up with soil to keep them through the winter. I never saw them frost caught, although we had much harder winters in those days than we do now.

From "Recalling the Past" by George Evans

We'd store root vegetables by piling them up in straw and covering them with thick earth – a tump. When there were no vegetables about you could open your tump and they'd be as fresh as the day you put them there and the soil would have kept the frost off.

Emily Griffiths

The trouble with a tump, though, was that you couldn't watch it day and night, and you couldn't lock it up..........!

The field by the pool, we used to plough him. The one year we grew halves. The one side was half potatoes and the other half swedes. Dad used to sell so many of the potatoes. Then one year we'd got so many left he was going to open the tump to sell some and when he went to open up the tump it all fell in a ruck! A bloke that used to live up there he was a beggar he'd been and pinched all the potatoes out of there.

Gordon Cook

We'd kill an owd fat lamb by sticking him through the ears with a knife then we'd skin and gut 'im. Our mum used to cure the skin, wash it and get a sack bag and stitch round it. It used to make a lovely rug. We used to have it upstairs I can see 'em now those old sheepskins. There was no fridges or none of that, we'd have to put it all down in salt in a big stein, a layer of salt and a layer of mutton, a layer of salt and so on like, until the stein was full.

Then we had another big owd stein full of nothing but home-cured lard that we had off the pig because we killed two pigs a year. That would do us for baking and cooking – lovely on toast this owd lard was, put some salt on it – it was lovely!

Heber Rowson

For the remote villages of the Stiperstones, travelling salesmen provided an important service.

We had our groceries delivered from M P Jones & Son of Pontesbury, with a horse and large box trap. He must have had about twenty of these horses and traps as he supplied the villages for miles around. A day or two before delivery, a Mr Harry Lakelin would come around on a push bike, taking the orders for next month's groceries and collecting the money for last month.

From "Recalling the Past" by George Evans

There was a man who used to come up, [to The Bog] and he used to take our monthly order. We used to pay once a month. It was Mr M P Jones from Pontesbury, also Bennetts came from Pontesbury and Roberts' came from Minsterley.

Our butcher used to come from Bishops Castle, Mrs Bowen. She used to come in a horse and trap and she'd start serving from Bishops Castle and then come to The Bog, so we'd have whatever was spare once everyone had had theirs. That was once a week.

I always remember Mr Lakelin used to come for our monthly order, which might include sugar, tea, margarine, flour and yeast for the baking. Mother always used to say, "It's Lakelin's week this week, you've got to be careful because we're at the end of everything!"

Sarah Ann Evans

Sometimes we'd have oats for our tea as we called it – that was porridge for our tea. That was a red letter day. On the day you paid your bill you always had something special. It could be a tin of salmon, it could be a tin of tomatoes, it could be a tin of peaches or half a pound of nice biscuits. Something special on that day but only that day.

Mollie Rowson

Mr M P Jones, the grocer from Pontesbury is also remembered for his generosity.

He was generous and let off poor debtors with half payment, and, since bread was cheaper if broken, he would allow his assistants to break it and give it cheaply.
From "The History of Minsterley" by Miss D T Merry.

When the mines closed (at The Bog) there were a lot of people owing money and Mr M P Jones wiped the slate clean. People didn't forget that, he must have been owed a lot of money.
Sarah Ann Evans

There were shops from Plox Green to The Bog

In the days when transport was not as readily available as it is today, each village and hamlet would be served by its own shops.

There were shops from Plox Green to The Bog. There was one up under the Devil's Chair that used to be kept by the Bettons, and there was Mrs Williams' and Mrs Swain The Bog. Mr Smitham kept the Tankerville shop. There was Albert Evans and his shop. There was Central Stores. There was John Davies' and there was Miss Molly Wardman's. They were all shops that you could buy from.
Mollie Rowson

Molly Wardman's shop.

At The Bog there was Mrs Ada Swain who kept the shop. It was a tiny little shop that sold almost everything and they used to have paraffin in the shed outside, she sold everything – a bit of grocery, sweets, almost everything. It was one of those little general stores, only a small place but packed. We used to go there with a ha'penny for sweets.
Millie Gough

Mrs Ada Swain had a shop at The Bog. Cigarettes, pipe tobacco and twist would be the main sale. Tobacco was mostly 'John Peel' and 'Tom Moody', both wrapped in special paper in a roll and twist, which you would see the old miners cut up with a very sharp knife and rub in their hands to put in their pipes. Some of them would chew a lump. Cigarettes were mostly 'Woodbines' and 'Players Navy Cut'.
From "Recalling the Past" by George Evans

For Ruth Chesters, Molly Wardman's 'emporium' at Snailbeach took some beating – especially at Christmas.

If I had a penny I'd go to Mr Davies' shop and I'd have a ha'penny worth of sweets and bring a ha'penny change back home. Mr Davies' shop had a bay window. He had various tins in this window, mainly sweets in jars. You could get a loaf of bread and you could get some sugar. I can't remember him ever selling milk. He didn't have great quantities of things only a bit. I used to go every morning with the milk can for a pint of milk. I can't remember the shops selling milk. But Molly Wardman's was great! You could get anything there. At Christmas time if you wanted to do some Christmas shopping she'd come and unlock late at night. She'd sell crockery and all things like that and she had the "Cosy Cafe" where you could have bread and butter, jam and cakes. Nothing was ever hot.
Ruth Chesters

'New fangled' items could present something of a challenge ....

There was Jack and Jimmy's [Mr Davies'] up the Shop Road. They used to fetch all the supplies in a basket on a Saturday from Shrewsbury. They used to have a little patch down behind the Village Hall and sell potatoes in the shop. The shelves weren't stacked out with food, there was plenty of shelves with plenty of room on them.

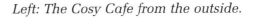

I remember the first banana we ever had. We had it from Parry's, the Central Stores, and we didn't know what to do with this banana so we ate it with the peel on, and then they told us we had got to take the peel off.

Doug Boulter

Eunice Davies used to sell milk in Snailbeach, when she gave up I took it on. I used to take nine to ten gallon down around Snailbeach delivering it everyday including Christmas Day. It was double the price you got from the creamery. Audrey used to wash and sterilise the bottles, that was almost a full time job. I bought an ex-army truck to deliver it with.

Wallace Evans

For those living in the more remote hamlets, provisions had to be carried considerable distances – by hand.

I can remember the kiddies as lived over Blakemoorgate, they'd come down for groceries and carry 'em all the way up – have so much this side their shoulder and so much that. And when we were children, after we come from school we went up to the top there and fetched milk for a penny a tin – skimmed milk.

Elsie Williams

Norman Ellis, the Minsterley butcher, would call on my father at the Gravels Post Office to see if he'd got a hare or summat and my father'd say, "Give me an hour or so", and when he came back from the Grit my father'd have it all ready.

Jim Booth

The morning shift at the mines commenced at six and so the miner started his day boiling the kettle. Coal was an expensive commodity and a 'flash' fire was often made using dried heather or gorse sticks in the grate.

With regard to the hills, we seemed to be a part of them and we used them for whatever purpose we required. A lot of people would fill a shed full of stalks of heather where they were left on the hill when the heather had been burned. These were used to light the kitchen fire.

From "Recalling the Past" by George Evans

We couldn't afford any coal. We used a lot of gorse sticks in the grates, thorn trees, mountain ash and heather sticks three-quarters of an inch thick.

Henry Jones

Every morning before my dad went to work, he'd have a basin full of what they used to call a 'basin of sup' - tea sup. It's the bread put into your basin and perhaps a bit of cheese cut into it and then make your tea, put some sugar on it and pour that all over it. Some milk and mix all that up. And I like it to this day.

Nellie Rowson

Breakfast for Sarah Ann Evans' family consisted of......

bacon and bread dipped in the fat and porridge.

In a miner's cottage food had to be prepared to sustain the workers throughout their long shift.

Strong smelling foods were rarely taken underground due to the confined working conditions. Nothing with a strong smell such as tinned salmon would be taken as 'bait'. A meat-pan full of home-cured bacon cooked in the side oven and left to go cold was a common sandwich filler. With the fat spread on the bread, slices of bacon and cheese would be added. Another trick was to gouge out a 'well' in a thick crust and fill this with butter.

Home-baked cakes and pies, again cooked in the side oven or in summer months in the frying pan. Welsh cakes were always a favourite item. If one had a baker's oven then cakes and pies would be taken out after the bread was part baked, giving rise to the saying if someone was simple minded that they had "Bin put in 'ooth the bread an brought out 'ooth the cakes!" Home made jam was a boon when not much else was available.

Large 'Bobby's Feet' of cheese and bacon or jam turnovers were cut into nice portions for use underground. Bread pudding was made into thick juicy chunks and sandwiches could be toasted if the 'cabin' or changing room had a fireplace or what they called a 'Rodney' which was a brazier with holes. Bottles of cold tea were the most usual beverage.

Emily Griffiths

My dad would be at Huglith Mines for six o'clock in the morning and work all day underground and finish at two. And I always remember in those days we had the very big

loaves of bread – cottage loaves – with a hole in the middle and there was a lovely crust down the one side, a soft crust, and me mum used to cut a big crust off the side of the loaf and there'd be a bit of bacon, a bit of cheese and then the other piece of bread she'd cut off again and put on the top of that. He'd have two big lumps to take to work and they'd be in a red and white hankerchief in those days – a red hankie with white spots on it.

Nellie Rowson

Meanwhile back at the cottage the rest of the family had to eat.

Hasty pudding was made hanging a pot of skimmed milk over the fire and mixing into it a cupful or so of plain flour and a little salt. Nourishing and filling. But I hardly imagine today's children giving it a welcome as we did.

Kettle broth was also a filling meal. Here we had bread broken into a basin, a few chopped chives, a lump of bacon fat or beef dripping (both plentiful in those days) and hot water poured over the lot. Kettle broth.

Well, sneer if you may but still better than the diet of the workhouse where so many of my parents' generation ended their pitiful lives.

From the diaries of Bill Francis published under the title "Hasty Pudding and Kettle Broth".

There were two kinds of Hasty Pudding, another name for it was Stir Pudding. Put some self raising flour into a bowl, mix it into a stiff dough with water. They would have a pan prepared with boiling water with salt in it. They would drop this lump of dough into it and it would cook. They'd lift it out with forks, put it on a dish, break it open and put butter and brown sugar in it. And you can believe me or not that is very good, it really is!

Emily Griffiths

We used to go fishing of course [in the River Onny] *leaning over the side of the brook and putting our hands under the turf at the side to get the fish out. We never got many, only small ones, half a pound would be a big trout.*

John Francis

Not a lot of people kept bees, not until later years and then they kept a few around Snailbeach, but we used to have a few.

Johnny Roberts

Everybody brewed, everybody baked

Thursday was baking day. They used to bake bread in this big bath and it would do us for the week. It didn't go stale. It would be a bit hard but we didn't get indigestion like we do today.

Sarah Ann Evans

One day of the week was baking day and mum used to bake with one of these baking ovens that you put the fire in a hole in the wall. They used sticks from the hedge brushings and you'd light the fire in the oven and keep on feeding it all the while and it would turn black. It was all like fire brick and they went black and you had to keep feeding it and feeding it and then they all went white with heat. Then you let it die down and scraped all the ashes out, mum wiped it around with the mop so we didn't have too much ash. But we put our bread on enamel plates, some used to put the bread straight on the bottom but you would get bits of cinder, bits of wood and that in it and that was horrible. Mum used to make two to three big cakes. The bread was made in one of those zinc baths that very often we kids would have a bath in but I think she kept a special one for the bread. When it rose it would be right up above the bath and she'd knock it down and knead it and it would rise up again and she'd knead it into these big loaves enough to last us a week.

Millie Gough

My grandparents used to live at the Rock Farm. They used to bake bread there. They used to collect heather to burn in the oven to heat the bricks up. You set fire to this heather and it would burn away and draw up the chimney. Of course before they put the bread in they had to sweep all the ashes out with a broom. Then they would put the bread in, close the door and bake it. When the bread was baked they would take it out and put the cakes in because the temperature then had fallen.

John Francis

A reputation as a skilled cook was to be cherished, and would spread for miles around as Gordon Cook remembers of life at Blakemoorgate:

They used to carry the wood up out of Gittinshaye to keep the baking oven going 'cos the owd lady was always baking. They used to carry timber up – great big owd oak stuff as had been there – down – years dead. Carry it up and saw it up and there'd be piles of logs and the owd lady used to do all this baking. Oh, talk about cakes and bread – there was nothing to touch it.

At the Harvest Festival the folks used to come from miles there to buy this bread and the owd lady's cakes.

Gordon Cook

It was all hard work in them days – patting up the butter. We used to sell it to Challinor's at Pontesbury – what we didn't want. There's nothing like real butter. It was beautiful. We did everything. We killed pigs. I used to make the pork pies, sausages, black puddings – everything. It was all work though.

Nora Pinches

As well as food, drink was often home-made and the ingredients used harvested from the hedgerows and fields.

We used to go picking cowslips. My mother used to make wine with them. Beautiful it was. She used to make wine with everything – dandelion wine, cowslip wine, elderberry and there is a nice wine you can make with the flowers.

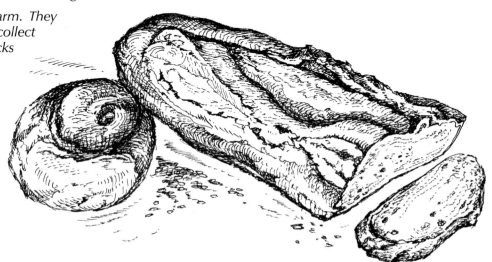

My mother made ginger beer. She had a big jar – bigger than a sweet jar. You put ginger in and some sugar and yeast and fill up this big jar. And every week she used to strain it off and we'd drink it. It was lovely. It's a lovely drink really.

Nora Pinches

We had a drink what they called 'Bees Wine'. We had a big glass jar and they'd put this stuff in it almost like yeast and a bit of sugar and these things used to work up and down and they'd grow. Then of course they'd go and give someone else some of it and they'd start one off. It was very sweet.

Sarah Ann Evans

The pig was treated as one of the family

If there is one thread common to almost all the memories recorded for 'Never on a Sunday', it is the importance of the pig to family life and survival. Most families seem to have kept one or more pigs, fed with every scrap of waste produced by the household, mixed with meal and bran. Seemingly almost a member of the family, the pig was thus fattened ready in due course for slaughter.

The killing was often carried out by a local man, experienced in the somewhat gory task, who provided the service for local households. It was an important service, carried out to a careful procedure, with a degree of ceremony and, above all, in a way designed to ensure that not a single part of the animal was wasted. There was, of course some sadness at the loss of a familiar 'friend', but in this way the pig helped to ensure there was food on the table for many months to come.

Pork pies, sausages, brawn, jelly from the trotters, black puddings from the blood, liver, 'lights', lard, scratchings....... so every part of the animal was put to use. "You can use every part of a pig – except the squeal!" ran the old, familiar line.

Tom Oldfield would go to the market and buy a bellyful of pigs, [a litter], and then he'd sell them around the village. You had two, you fed one up 'til he was a porker and then you went round the village and got orders. When others killed their pig you ordered a piece off them. The pig was treated as one of the family. I've stirred the blood – if it wan't being used it had to go around the rhubarb.

Johnny Butler

The re-use of household waste to feed the pig would be called re-cycling in modern parlance. Though the smell it emitted was not the most pleasant, the end result made it all worth while.

Outside by the toilet was all the tubs of pig wash. Everything you had went in the pig-wash in those days, even your washing-up water went into those tubs and anything gone-off they all went in that. Oh, and it used to smell terrible. All the vegetables and all the waste went into the pig-wash and then they'd mix so much bran or meal in a bucket and they'd get a couple of scoops of this stuff out of the tubs and mix it all up together and put it in a big long trough for the pigs to eat out of. And do you know what, you never had pork tasting as nice these days as you did then.

Nellie Rowson

For young children, the sight of the family pig being slaughtered – necessary though it was – could be an upsetting spectacle.

I didn't like it when the pig was killed. I was only seven or eight and was always scratching its head, and then to see him being tied up on a bench and have his throat cut and to hear him screaming his head off, well, it used to make me feel quite ill.

John Bennett

We killed two pigs every year. We had the pork and everything. Oh, it was nice. I didn't like to see him killed though after feeding him. There'd got to be an 'R' in the month when you killed your pig.

George Balmer

I used to disappear the day they killed the pig. I used to go as far up the hill as I could go so I couldn't hear it screaming.

Sybil Cook

Nevertheless, it was a notable occasion which stayed long in the memory.

It was a day's job killing a pig – beer and wine. It was a real feast to kill the pig.

Roly Johnson

I remember pig killing day and getting the boiler going. You had to pay the man who came to kill the pig, it wouldn't be much, there wasn't the money about. When they cut the pig up they cut down the back and cut the 'chine' (backbone) into pieces, and you'd give that to your neighbours. And when they killed their pig they'd come and give you a piece of theirs.
Sarah Ann Evans

Virtually every part of the pig could be, and was, eaten. The bladder, however, was eagerly sought after by children – for other purposes.

When you killed the pig its throat was slit and you got a bucket to collect the blood. Then you had to stir it 'til it went cold. Out of the blood you would make black puddings. The intestines were used for the black puddings. Everything was used, the liver, the heart, the kidneys, the tongue would be pressed, the head turned into brawn, the tail and the trotters. The bladder could be used for a football. It was all kept on the cold slab until it was eaten. Hams and bacons would be hanging from hooks in the kitchen.
Doug Boulter

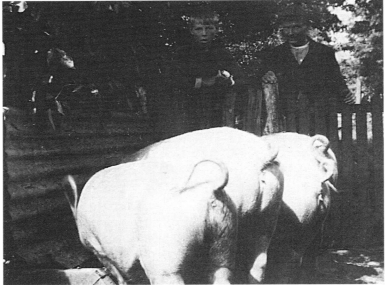
The pig was treated as one of the family.

We couldn't wait for the bladder to go cold so as we could play football. It would last for ages.
Millie Gough

I used to have to stir the blood to make the black puddings. I would take the bowels down in the brook at Lower Hogstow to wash, turning them on a stick and you keep turning them two or three times until they are clean.
The bowels were in what you used to call the 'veil', it was like a fat. You cut that up and made faggots with that.
Betty Hordley

Well known expressions which we use regularly today often have their origins in the routines and events of household life for past generations.

They cut the pig's throat and let it bleed to death which was quite gruesome and then they hung it up on what they called the gambrol, hung it up by its back feet – years and years ago that used to be called the bucket. Hence the expression, 'Kick the bucket', because when the pig actually dies the nerve makes them give a final kick and he would kick the gambrel with his back feet and they called it kicking the bucket.
Connie Read

Salt has been used for seasoning and, more importantly, preserving meat and other items since time immemorial. Right up until the time when refrigerators became common, salt and other preservatives continued to play a vital role in almost every household.

It, [the pig], was put in what you'd call the 'cooler' - a bacon box with two sides for two hams and you used to put saltpetre on it to start with and then salt. You used to buy the bars in six pound blocks and break that up and put it in a pan in front of the fire to make sure there were no lumps in it. It was a nightmare of a job. If it was in for a month, you'd turn it at the fortnight – bring the bottom flitch up to the top. When it had been there a month, take it out, wash all the salt off it and hang it up on hooks. Then if it was a very hot summer, you'd get blow fly maggots. They used to put him in a very fine muslin bag. But I know one person who used to whitewash it and that sealed all the cracks.
Roly Johnson

It was a tricky job if you didn't do it properly, you could lose the lot. It could be twelve months before you cut into a ham, we used to put pillow cases over ours else you get a blow fly in it and a maggot or two. Mind you, they said in them days it was a better ham if you'd got a blow fly in it! There'd be a rack 'above the house' with hams on just drying slowly.

We used to put butter down in salt in steins. You'd cut it out and soak it to get the salt out and it would be like it was real fresh. They'd do beans and things the same way.

Wilfred Andrews

I could remember how my mother used to salt it. She crushed up block salt and where the veins were she always rubbed those with saltpetre and then she sprinkled brown sugar lightly all over before she put the salt on, a fair thickness of salt which would turn to brine. After ten days the cheeks used to come out – they were very sweet. The flitches came out at about three weeks, they was lovely pictures hung up on the wall! The hams were about a month.

Wallace Evans

Mum used to salt the pig on the floor in the dairy and we girls weren't allowed to go near – because of the old wives' tale that when you had a period you were 'unclean'. Your mum never salted a pig when she had a period – never! And we girls, when we came to that age were NOT allowed anywhere near it. They reckoned that the pig wouldn't take the salt and it wouldn't keep!

Millie Gough

Mother bought a piece of bacon every week – I can see it now, about two pounds of bacon in a piece and you cut at that every day. We hung that piece of bacon 'over the house' [usually refers to above the fireplace], *peppered it, and hung it 'over the house', it wasn't in the pantry it was hung on a nail 'over the house'!*

Mollie Rowson

The (pig) fat was made into lard, scratchings. That was all melted down and mother used to use that for baking. It was taken out and cut up into chunks and put in the pan over the fire and boiled up and stirred and when all the fat was out of it, drained off through a colander and stuck in whatever they were going to put it in. Then when it came baking day, you had to cut a piece out.

Roly Johnson

When I was in my teens and used to go up to the Rowson's to play darts and dominoes and cards and sing for hours, many's the time I've come home and got the flitch down and cut two or three slices off and had it on the toasting fork in front of the fire and let the fat drip onto the bread – it was marvellous.

Wallace Evans

We'd make the jelly out of the trotters and brawn out of the spare pork. It was nicer than you can buy today. It was the real thing wasn't it? Same with the sausages. I used to make the sausages and all the puddings of the pig, the small ones. You used to always have somebody to pour the water and to turn them all – put 'em round your fingers and turn 'em and let 'em go straight through till they were turned all inside out. That's how you cleaned 'em. They were lovely and clean after and then you'd make them into sausages.

Nora Pinches

The liver would be hung outside on a nail to cool and it would be in the pan almost before the pig had gone cold and we would be eating it with gravy and onions.

Millie Gough

When the Second World War necessitated rationing ....

You could be in more trouble for killing your pig on the wrong day than killing your wife – you had to have a permit – from the Ministry of Agriculture Inspectorate. You'd get away with killing your wife much easier.

Connie Read

Chapels and churches of the area

(clockwise from top left)
Lordshill Chapel
Snailbeach Methodist Church
The Ore House (the Baptists' winter meeting place)
Pennerley Chapel
Snailbeach Methodist Church
St Luke's Church, Snailbeach
The old Perkins Beach Chapel

3: Holy! Holy! Holy!

If one theme dominates the memories of older generations of Stiperstones folk, it is how special and distinct Sunday was. From Monday to Saturday there was time for little else but work, whether it be paid employment or in the home, garden or small-holding. Sunday, however - the Lord's day - was different. No work took place unless it was absolutely necessary. Animals were fed, cows milked, but little else. In many homes, no reading material was allowed other than the Bible and the Christian Herald and often three separate journeys were made to the local chapel for services and Sunday School. It is even recorded that a Mr Lakelin from Pontesbury, who was Methodist Pastor for Snailbeach in the 19th century, stayed up until midnight on Saturday to feed his horse and then made it fast until midnight on Sunday. Despite these imposed rigours, it is said the horse faithfully carried him to three services each Sunday at Minsterley, Wrentnall and Snailbeach!

As in many other mining districts, nonconformism took a strong hold from the early years of the 19th century onwards. The arrival of mining families from Cornwall and South Wales, seeking work at the fast developing lead mines, would have given a timely boost to an embryonic free-church movement which had certainly reached Minsterley by the 1790s. Baptists were meeting at a house in Snailbeach by 1803, had become a separate church by 1818 and, after 15 years of meeting in the local blacksmith's shop, built their own chapel on Lordshill in 1833. Attempts were made to hold regular Methodist services in the village in 1840 and a permanent Methodist congregation had been established there by 1859. The Methodist chapel in Snailbeach was finally built in 1876 on land leased from the Marquis of Bath for ten shillings per year. At the same time, other chapels were being established at Pennerley and Perkins Beach and a Meeting House on the edge of the Stiperstones at the Paddock (now long closed). St. Luke's Anglican church was built in 1872 on the far side of Minsterley parish, just inside the village of Snailbeach, as an early example of 'church planting'. This 'mission' church, however, seems to have had only limited success initially and was closed for long periods. One member of the local clergy recorded a terse note in the register, that the church, "... has unfortunately been closed on and off owing to the utter indifference of the people up here".

The mine managers, or 'captains' as they were known, often seem to have played an important role in encouraging the establishment of local nonconformist congregations and the building of chapels for them. Henry Dennis, appointed to manage the Snailbeach mine in 1870, helped to persuade the then Marquis of Bath to lease land for the Methodist chapel at Snailbeach and also contributed no small amount towards the cost of its erection. The Marquis (from Longleat) was one of the major landowners in the Stiperstones area at the time. His family were known, however, as being 'high church', with no great love for the growing free-church movement in the Stiperstones mining villages and the story goes that an earlier Marquis had refused point blank to allow the Baptists to build on his land. Undeterred, they approached another local landowner, Lord Tankerville, in the hope that a recent dispute with the Marquis over shooting rights might make him more sympathetic. Sure enough, Lord Tankerville provided land for Lordshill Chapel to be built – just across the stream which formed the boundary between his land and that of the Marquis.

The local chapels grew in strength, and probably reached their peak in the later years of the 19th century and in the early years of the 20th. They met not only a spiritual and moral need, but also a social one. People's memories of their childhood and early years are full of references to Harvest Festivals, Camp Meetings, Sunday School trips, anniversaries and concerts. Local churches and chapels provided an important focus for the life of the communities they served, and earned an undisputed place in the affections of their congregations.

Sunday was a busy day

Sunday was a busy day, it really was. We started on the Sunday morning at half past ten – Sunday School. Well from there we came back home about half past eleven and if mum was lucky enough in the summer to have a little bit of meat (it usually used to be a shoulder of lamb, breast of lamb or something like that), she'd dip us some bread in it and that was lovely. Just a piece to last 'til dinner time, it was nice.

We'd have our dinner and go back to Sunday School again for half past one. We used to have cards with a stamp on and they'd stamp your card every time you went. There used to be two chaps stamping your card in the bottom window by the door there.

Then after that we daren't come home, we had to stop for chapel at a quarter to three.

Back in chapel again at six o'clock. Then there was a collection. Mum and dad gave 2d each. We kids gave a penny. That was the collection, on a brass plate, it used to rattle. Mind you that was a lot of money from our house, with four children.

After that mum and dad were in the choir, so they stayed for practice. We were there 'til nine o'clock!

Back home we'd come at nine o'clock at night. When we got in the house it used to smell nice, because what we'd have for dinner – the leftovers and all the nice vegetables – were put in the oven by the side of the fire before we went to chapel. There wouldn't be a big fire and those would be smelling lovely when you came in. You'd have a little bit of that on a tea plate, perhaps a little bit of bread and butter and off to bed with a candle.

Mollie Rowson

SERVE THE LORD WITH GLADNESS
TEXT BEHIND THE PULPIT IN THE CHAPEL

LORDSHILL BAPTIST CHAPEL

There have been Baptists in the district for around 200 years. The Lordshill Baptist church was built on the slopes of the Stiperstones a little way out of the village of Snailbeach. Peggy Chidley remembers that it attracted a congregation from a wide area.

There was more people I've heard dad say used to come down the road from the Vessons. You'd see their lamps, oil lamps, coming. Dad used to reckon there was almost as many people came from over the back side of the hill as there was went from the village.

Peggy Chidley

The Minsterley Methodist Circuit at one time comprised some thirteen small places of worship under one minister. The chapels at Snailbeach, Perkins Beach and Pennerley are situated within a few miles of each other along the Stiperstones range and are sometimes referred to as "the three hillside Methodist churches". The circuit also included a meeting place at The Paddock, a now deserted mining hamlet on the upper slopes of the Stiperstones.

Events and special services were organised throughout the year by the chapels.

Each of the chapels closed their own place for the special occasions of the other two. One such occasion would be a Camp Meeting when four or five preachers had been selected (to preach, often in the open). The congregation, singing lustily, paraded around the area to the chosen camp ground. Today, only Perkins Beach continues the custom, which originated in America. There was a meeting house at The Paddock over the top of the Stiperstones. I used to walk across as a child with twenty to thirty people to their camp meetings. Harvest Festivals too were of special significance, people bringing the choicest of farm and garden produce. A weeknight sale of produce and supper formed part of the festival and in early years, rabbit pie was the main dish for the supper.

Emily Griffiths

The preachers often preached in the open and the congregation sang lustily

We used to have a Harvest Festival at The Paddock. The Paddock meeting house was a chapel. They'd come for miles. Then there used to be a Camp Meeting and they used to walk from Snailbeach, The Bog, Habberley. There were crowds there. It was a service as they used to have three or four preachers at – preaching and singing, like. It was alright.

Gordon Cook

I have known them to have the open air service up on the mine site where the steps are [the engine house opposite George's shaft]. *The preacher would get up on the steps and that would be his pulpit and we'd all sit on the grass.*

Susie Hartshorn

Mollie Wardman used to come to our church at St Luke's. She would give to the Methodists, well she used to attend the Methodists as well, and the Baptists, the Jehovah Witnesses and the Salvation Army. The Reverend Morson said to her one morning in church, "Mollie, you're like the old town sow – you go everywhere!" But she was a smashing woman.

Bernard Millington

Not even the shoes were cleaned on a Sunday

For the majority of people in the area the Sabbath was primarily a day of worship. Only those tasks considered absolutely essential would be carried out, and as Ruth Chesters indicates in the above quote the list of tasks was tightly drawn.

You never worked on a Sunday. The only jobs done were those that had to be done, like milk the cows and feed, them but the last thing you would do would be to get the horses and go out and work! I remember, it must have been in my teens, we lost a lovely field of hay. It was all ready to get in and we could have got it quite easily on the Sunday. But there was a thunderstorm and we never got it and it was there for about seven weeks and the grass had grown up all around it.

Jack Pugh

My dad was real chapel. He wouldn't let us sew on a Sunday, they never used to in them days, you know. He was very strict about that.

Nora Pinches

The Paddock Meeting House was a chapel. They used to come from miles around.

You did as least as possible on a Sunday. My grandfather was a Primitive Methodist preacher and he had a smallholding and the only thing he did on a Sunday was to milk the cow and feed the chickens. His boots were always clean, but he never cleaned his boots or never did anything other than the jobs that were necessary, like the milking and feeding, and went to chapel after that. That was an all-day job like a wedding was, and a funeral was about as good!
Roly Johnson

Even reading material was restricted on a Sunday.

You were not allowed to do anything on a Sunday. Mum got the dinner, but as far as a newspaper – the only newspaper my dad ever read on a Sunday was the Christian Herald. Before we went to bed dad always read a chapter out of the Bible to us.
Nellie Rowson

Granny was very, very, good, she did nothing on a Sunday. She wouldn't peel the potatoes on a Sunday, the newspaper called the Wellington Journal was put up on a Saturday night and you didn't see that 'til Monday evening. We weren't allowed to play with a ball on a Sunday. All you could do was look at a book or write something. Mind you, by the time you walked to Lordshill twice every Sunday to Sunday School, or maybe three times if we had to go back to the service at night with mum, we were up and down the Lordshill Bank like yo-yos.
Mary Challinor

Anybody who dared to break the unwritten rule risked serious social disapproval.

I remember Mrs Rowson telling me off because I pegged Joe's napkins [nappies] out on the Sunday and Mary had done hers, she'd hung 'em up in the house, like, 'cos Mr Price might see 'em when they were going to chapel. It was such a disgrace to do your washing on a Sunday. Got into trouble I did for that. Mary's mother, Mrs Rowson, told me that when her father was alive, she had to do the potatoes and everything like that on a Saturday night. The last thing she did was do the front step 'cos she wasn't allowed to do it on a Sunday.
Elsie Rowson

This way of life was handed down, unquestioned, from generation to generation.

It was a thing that was done by your parents and they had been brought up with it. The last war changed all that!
Jack Pugh

Chapels were very, very, poor looking

Chapels were mainly modest and unadorned. Services were often lengthy and fervent with the main emphasis on preaching. The congregation listened attentively and responded zealously with "Amen", "Praise the Lord" and "Alleluia".

Chapels were very, very, poor looking . They were simple and stark, just scrubbed wooden floors and just whitewashed or colourwashed walls, and very simple seats which were very uncomfortable, but that didn't matter. At Snailbeach Methodist Chapel, underneath the seats, there are special wooden slats which were put there for the miners to put their top hats on. And that is unique, I have never seen it anywhere else.

Emily Griffiths

Mary Webb, in her novel *The Golden Arrow*, describes a local Methodist Chapel, capturing its simplicity and austerity.

Whatever beauty flowered within to sweeten the stark ugliness of it – creeping up the walls like swift summer vetches, reaching out determined tendrils towards the illimitable – none was visible without..... it was squat, with round-topped windows too large and too many for it..... Its paint was of the depressing colour known among house painters as Pompeian red. The windows had black rep curtains and frosted lower panes to defend the young women in the window pews from the eyes that came up above the window-sills at dusk like stars, when the unrighteous outside stood on a ledge and pressed their faces to the glass. So the chapel stood amid the piled and terraced hills like a jibe. Above the door, with a nervous and pardonable shuffling of responsibility (apparently by the architect) were the words, 'This is the Lords' Doing'.

Everybody had a new suit for the anniversary

Children in particular looked forward to occasions such as the Sunday School anniversary and the 'treats'.

The annual Sunday School anniversary was a red letter day, when children sang and recited with the chapel choir. Following this a tea party was held. Each chapel had its waitresses, lady members being responsible for their table and bringing their own snowy tablecloths and treasured best china tea services. The feast consisted of white and brown bread and butter, and possibly three kinds of slab cake. Simple, but to the children of the village as good as nectar and ambrosia. After the tea there was a scramble for nuts and sweets donated by a local shopkeeper.

Emily Griffiths

Snailbeach Sunday School circa 1910.

Everybody had a new suit for the anniversary. Mother prided herself that up 'til the time I left school she never paid more than a quid for my suit.

Johnny Butler

One anniversary I remember – you always had new clothes for the Sunday School anniversary, Mum hadn't got any money, she didn't know what she was going to do and Uncle Walter lent her £5 to buy us something for the anniversary, and she slowly paid it back.

Mollie Rowson

Our highlights of the year I suppose, were the chapel. Because it was on a Good Friday, the Baptists had their march round the village and ended up at Parry's, the Central [shop], where we had the scramble for sweets and nuts. There used to be about three buckets of sweets and nuts. They used to take the little ones off on one side with a basketful and we used to scramble for these sweets. And on a Whit Monday it was the Methodists' turn and we had a Field Day, we had games in the field and all the rest of it after the tea, and we really liked that better, you know, as kids!

Elsie Rowson

Snailbeach Sunday School Anniversary 1999

Sunday School trips were also organised annually – sometimes to the seaside but sometimes to a more local destination.

Sunday School outing to Happy Valley, Pontesford, early 1900's

We used to have a trip once every twelve months, up to Corndon, walk up to the top of Corndon. Aah, that was the trip – sweets, apples and oranges. And we used to have 'treats', that was held at the Knapp that's where the Sunday School treats was held.

Roly Johnson

Sunday School was a central part of each Sunday for most children. Regular attendance was considered important and was monitored closely – and rewarded.

You were brought up in chapel. There was Sunday School in the morning and Sunday School in the afternoon. Some kids had to stay behind for the service. The registers show that there was nobody missing. If you were sick you sent a note. It was real regimental like.
I often think about the little kids singing ....

> *What can wash away my sin*
> *Nothing but the mark of Jesus........*

Those poor little kids!

Johnny Butler

The Church was the most important thing in my parents' lives. My dad was superintendent at the Sunday School. I was only a little girl about four when he took me with him across to the Sunday School.

Ruth Chesters

We used to have little tickets for going to Sunday School, for being there. And when we got about ten of them, we'd have a big picture, a Bible picture to put in an album.

Nora Pinches

I once went down the Hopyard with Fred Lewis of Gorsty Bank to pick some nuts instead of going to chapel. Well, I was frightened to death in case our mum and dad got to know . Terrified, I came home with these few nuts and didn't know where to hide them. I hid them under a stone up the path. I thought whatever will they say? I'd never been to church. I'd been nutting!

Mollie Rowson

For a young Nellie Rowson, curiosity about the Sunday School her brothers and sisters were attending proved too much.

I was very, very shy and I do remember once, I decided I could go to the Sunday School on my own. The others had gone so I walked up the Crowsnest bank, down the line and the little short cut up to the chapel. But I was too shy to go in. I always remember hiding behind a gravestone until one of our teachers, Flossie Evans, was coming and she spotted me there. I was too shy to go into chapel, so she took me in.

Nellie Rowson

Church and chapel activities were not restricted, however, to a Sunday.

I went to Sunday School up until I was eighteen and then I went in the choir. Your life was around that church all the time. After you'd had Sunday School there was Guild in the week. On a Friday night there was a Youth Fellowship in Minsterley. Perhaps there'd be sixteen of us. We would push-bike down there. It was Bible study one night and once a month we'd have a social evening.

Ruth Chesters

The Churching of Women

Until quite recently, it was customary for women to come to be 'churched' at their local church after giving birth to a child. It was generally accepted that a new mother would not visit anyone until this customary duty had been fulfilled. The service in the old Prayer Book was actually entitled 'The Thanksgiving of Women after Childbirth'. There was a simi-lar Methodist service called 'The Thanksgiving of Mothers'. The custom derived its force not just from the natural desire to give thanks, but from a sense that a woman needed to be cleansed after childbirth before she could re-enter the normal round of social life.

Though the Reformation and the Book of Common Prayer brought in a change of emphasis to make it a ceremony of thanksgiving (very heartfelt, one would think, when so many mothers and infants died in or soon after childbirth), the old medieval idea of purification never disappeared in popular thought.

In practice, though, the tradition of churching has all but died out in recent years.

Reverend William Rowell

Snailbeach Methodist Chapel

However, the churching of women is still remembered by some today.

You'd got to be churched, it was quite a ritual, you were not thought to be very good after having babies and you had to be cleansed. It was almost compulsory.

Jean Lewis

It was offered to women, and it used to take place, but it was optional. You weren't made to have it done. I accepted it as a prayer of thanksgiving for a safe delivery of a baby. It made you feel good that you'd gone to the trouble and thought about Jesus.

It did get done at the Methodists as well as the Church.

Dorothy Trow

We had some wonderful singers

The choir played an important role in chapel life and the business of singing was taken very seriously.

Each little church had a choir, they would appoint a choir master, and they had the old pedal organs or harmoniums. But they all sang in parts, they took the four parts always. They would perhaps go and visit other chapels, if they had a good choir, perhaps over at the Grit or Norbury. But they'd walk, they'd think nothing of walking ten or twelve miles to give a concert somewhere.

Emily Griffiths

Mr William Purslow was at Clover House. He was still a Sunday School teacher when I went to Perkins Beach Sunday School. There was a Mr Edwin Jones who also lived at Mytton Dingle, he often held a prayer meeting after the evening service and all the older men would get real worked up, and I can remember Mr Jones would stamp the floor and shout, "Praise the Lord", and so forth at the top of his voice. The whole chapel would appear to be alive and rocking.

From "Recalling the Past" by George Evans

We'd all have to go to chapel and have our service and afterwards my mum and dad were in the choir. It'd be choir practice. I was only tiny, but I can remember after choir practice my dad would stand me on the seat in the chapel by the organ and roll me up in a plaid shawl to carry me home to the Crowsnest.

Nellie Rowson

Critical to the success of a choir was the choir-master (often the chapel organist). The post was a voluntary one, but well respected locally.

...........and of course Mr Joseph Evans, he was the organist. He's buried just outside the chapel doors there. I think sixty years he was organist. He started when he was twelve and he used to walk to Lordshill when he was young and then he had a cycle. He used to leave his bike there in the blacksmith's shop and walk up to Lordshill. He lived at one of the farms at Shelve.

We used to have what we called Joe's Concert. That was once a year and the proceeds was his wages for the year. We had a concert and oh we had some wonderful singers. I can hear 'em now. There was some wonderful voices – Welsh. I can hear 'em now.

Elsie Rowson

Mr Joseph Evans, the organist (front row, centre) with the rest of the Lordshill choir

4: To toil and not to seek for rest

Employment opportunities for people who lived in the isolated villages and hamlets along the Stiperstones in the earlier years of the last century were at best limited.

Young men and women leaving school at fourteen could look to earn a wage in the local mining industry, working on the land at one of the larger farms, or going 'into service', either nearby or perhaps in a large house in one of the cities such as Birmingham, Liverpool, or even London. Others with the necessary skills and aptitude might be lucky enough to sign up for an apprenticeship. Being time-served held out the prospect of a job virtually for life, but the apprenticeship itself could be long, hard and badly paid, (or even not paid at all). Those who 'broke' their apprentice-ships faced severe financial penalties. Many young people followed the same trade or line of work as their fathers before them – and often their grandfathers and great grand-fathers before that.

The Stiperstones lead mining industry had reached its height in the 1860s and '70s when in excess of a thousand men were employed locally. By the turn of the century, cheap imported lead had forced the price down. Many of the mines closed, others turned to the production of barytes – a dense white mineral with a rang of industrial uses. For a while, this alternative source of revenue allowed a number of mines to continue operating and even to develop. By the First World War, however, the mining era on the Stiperstones was drawing to a close. In the 1920s and '30s only a handful of mines were providing work locally. Notably amongst them was Huglith mine, near Habberley, which features extensively in many people's memories of the period.

The years between the wars were also, of course, a period of significant economic depression. The people of the Stiperstones area did not escape its effects. Many were forced to adjust to life 'on the dole'; queuing to collect their money weekly from specially established offices at Minsterley, and elsewhere. The expression 'means test' had a very real sense then. People were forced to sell virtually everything they had of value before they were allowed to collect what many still saw as a hand-out.

Transport had always been a problem for Stiperstones villagers, whether to collect the dole or get to work. Roads at one time were little more than dirt tracks, and personal motorised transport a considerable rarity and largely the province of the local gentry (and 'toffs'). People were accustomed to walking, or perhaps cycling many miles to get to work each day and then the same distance back at night. Often this was followed by an evening spent working on the family small holding or garden, in order to supplement a meagre wage and ensure food could be placed on the table for hungry mouths.

For a family to survive, it was necessary for every member to play their part. As soon as children became old enough to carry out simple tasks around the house, garden or farm they were allotted jobs which became their responsibility on a regular basis. The gathering of water and fuel were central to family life.

You had to work as soon as you could get about and you could lift and carry. All the kids had to work. Henry Jones

So many were still working on 'Black Tom' [a mine in Snailbeach], like. Well me mum made me a coarse apron and I used to go out and help them on washing the ore there and then I went into the cabin and had me bait, bread and cheese, with them. I wasn't really working I was only a little child. Elsie Williams

As children we had to walk around the fields in the springtime to pick stones. We had to take a bucket after school and pick stones. Bill Evans

My father died with TB which was then raging around the countryside so mother had to go out to work so many days a week to earn some money. As kids we earned money from whinberry picking, blackberry picking and cutting sticks. We'd bag sticks and sell them at a shilling or one and six a bag. Derek Rowson

Similarly, young teenagers soon became old enough to earn a living in their own right. Even a small wage could make a valuable contribution to the family income. Their tender years and lack of experience, however, could sometimes have humorous consequences.

Dad would go to Captain Oldfields' down the wood when he was a boy, as a house boy, and I can always remember him saying that when they were killing a chicken in those days what they had to do was get a block of wood, hold the chicken in their hand, get the block and cut the hen's head off. Dad put the chicken down and off it flew up in the wood. Peggy Chidley

I was a paper girl, only on a Saturday, delivering Reynolds newspapers and Wellington Journals. Mollie Rowson

Getting water from the well.

Wash day was always a Monday – we had a boiler outside in the shed. We had to carry the water from the well to fill the boiler and then get it boiling. There was a dolly tub and a mangle and our line was at the far end.

Sarah Ann Evans

Every Sunday I used to carry eighteen buckets of water to fill a thirty-six gallon cast iron boiler for mum to wash on a Monday and I had to gather all sorts of sticks to burn to heat the boiler because we couldn't afford the coal. Everybody collected firewood, heather sticks, tied up in a bundle on a wheel barrow.

Henry Jones

We had a very good dairy across the yard and then dad built a wash house as well. There was a boiler, you put the fire underneath and we'd have to carry fifteen buckets of water from the well to start to wash. You'd fill the boiler and fill the baths for rinsing. A dolly tub and a mangle used to come out. You'd be washing all day. We had these unbleached sheets and by the time we'd boiled them and blued them and boiled them and blued them they'd be as white as snow. I can remember pegging clothes on the line when it's been freezing them as hard while you've been doing it, but they've come in beautiful, smelling beautiful when they'd dried. But we would be washing all day.

Millie Gough

All day Monday was wash day. It was hard work. Then Tuesday was ironing day. They used these flat irons heated on the fire and if there was a bit of smoke in the fireplace they would get black and it wouldn't be very easy to get the black off them. If you could get a red glowing fire then the irons would get red hot. Wednesday would be cleaning day; the peg rugs would be shook. Black-leading the grate would take an hour or two. Thursday would be churning day, mum would be making butter to take to Bishops Castle market with the eggs on a Friday.

Brenda Jones

Whether the cow calved or the bull broke his neck Monday was washing day.

On a Monday morning mum liked to brush all the best clothes and put them away before she did anything else. That was while the boiler was getting hot ready for washing. She'd have all the best clothes down on the big top table brushing all those and folding them up. There was no hangers or wardrobes, she'd fold them up and put them away in a box ready for next Sunday.

We used a dolly tub and a peggy and you'd get it in the tub and bump and bump and twist it around. Then you'd get the washing out into a big zinc bath and scrub them with soap. Whites would then go into the boiler for boiling and be drawn out with a long wooden peg. It would all be rinsed through in cold water and then there'd be another bath of water with a dolly blue to make the whites whiter. Shirt collars had to be soaked and scrubbed.

Nellie Rowson

Mother took in washing, she washed for a doctor and a farm and there was eight of us kids. I don't know how she did it.

There was an old copper [wash boiler] you had to light the fire under and iron with an iron you put in the bars of the fire. I just don't know how she did it.

Bernard Millington

Mostly, every woman would wear what they called a rough apron, which they made out of a fine woven hessian sack, to do their washing and housework. Some of the floors of the houses were laid with stone flags and would be washed by the woman on her knees with a bucket of water and a mop cloth which was always called a floor cloth. Round the house was mostly laid with stone flags and had to be washed down at least once a week. It was usually a job for Saturday morning when bucket after bucket of water would have to be carried and thrown in front of the one who was doing the sweeping with a rough broom. It was usually a job for the children.

From "Recalling the Past" by George Evans

Butchering was an essential local trade. When the time came for the family pig to be slaughtered, men known in the area to be skilled in the task would often be hired for a small fee.

We had a small holding up the Ventor about ten acres. My father farmed on and off, he used to rear his own pigs and sheep and he used to kill them. By trade he was a butcher he used to go miles on horseback killing pigs, all out the Bridges around Darnford, out as far as the Gravels, Plox Green, Snailbeach. He might kill five or six pigs today, then he used to cut 'em up, and he would cure 'em, salt 'em and he would charge three shillings. My mother used to go out with dad on the pony and trap delivering meat.

Johnny Roberts

To gain an apprenticeship as a butcher was to have the opportunity to learn a valued trade. The 'terms and conditions' of employment, however, were not the most generous.

My first job was when they planted Gittinshaye, they planted it with firs. My first job, three or four of us used to do it,

Hilda Yapp, Snailbeach Farm Cottages early 1940's

was to go and cut the fern when it started to grow in the trees. We worked for a chap the name of Thomas, a Welsh chap, but it was sort of sub-let to him off Harrop. I didn't do that for long I can tell you. I wanted to go butchering. I was an apprentice butcher to Peter Edwards in Hanwood, he said I wouldn't get any money for it – so I didn't! I had to bike it from Pennerley. I was a 'bound apprentice' and in them days it was done through a solicitor. You had to pay, if you were a 'bound apprentice'. We'll say for the sake of argument it was £100 and if you broke your contract you had to pay him that £100.

Roly Johnson

The cattle market was on Smithfield Road in Shrewsbury and the village butchers would only buy what animals they were confident that they had orders for during the next week.

A chap, the name of Webster, used to drive them out (the animals) and he would get a few bob off Peter Edwards and the other butchers for doing it. He'd start from Shrewsbury to walk 'em all out – Peter Edwards from Hanwood would be the first off. Then he'd come on to Hignetts at Pontesbury, they'd be next and Norman Ellis at Minsterley would be the last. I tell you what that was a very, very touchy job, that was, driving animals, especially in the summer time in the heat, 'cos the beggars would get down on you. I tell you it'd be no good starting to cut 'em because they'd got to stop there 'til they'd got there wind back so as they could come on.

Roly Johnson

I was fourteen when I left school and went to work for a butcher as an errand boy, you learnt whatever you could. I worked for him for four years and had the sack thirteen times. I started with four bob a week and finished up getting seventeen bob, that's how I know I was sacked thirteen times 'cos every time he sacked me he'd give me a bob rise to come back.

On a Monday I'd be making sausages, pressed beef, brawn and black puddings. When you was boiling the black puddings it was twenty minutes and you'd got to put soda in the water. If you boiled them for twenty-one minutes and *they burst you'd have the sack. He brought you up that you'd got to take responsibility.*   Bernard Millington

Down in the valley, Minsterley was the nearest thing to a 'town' this side of Shrewsbury for the people of the Stiperstones. There were a number of shops and small businesses there which provided employment for local people. The establishment of a rail head in 1861 gave a significant boost to the local economy and led to a thriving coal yard next to the station which supplied homes over a wide area including the Stiperstones.

My dad was a miner. He used to walk to Huglith until he got this terrible silicosis. Then he used to do a lot of odd job work. He used to work on the coal filling the bags at Minsterley station. But he had hardly got the breath to push his bike back up the road his chest was so bad. Mum worked at Rea Valley (Canning Factory) when they tinned potatoes. She used to go cleaning to get extra money. When I left school at fourteen I was at home twelve months because dad was so poorly then. Eventually I went to work at the big house by the garage in Minsterley where the lady used to take boarders. Then I worked for Mrs Savage in the shop at Minsterley for seventeen years until my mum got ill.   Ruth Chesters

My brother Bert bought a lorry from David Oldfield and I drove that for a while delivering cattle food. One job I used to enjoy very much was when David used to take orders from the farmers for cider at harvest time, and I would go up to Bulmers in Hereford, fetch a load of barrels back and deliver around the farms. Almost all the farmers would have a barrel in for the harvest. I did this up until the war, then that put pay to the lorry and Bert went in the airforce.   Bill Evans

My dad used to lug the manure out for all the little holdings on the hill and cut 'em their hay. He would come and lug manure out for half a crown a day, with a horse and cart. Then he used to go to Minsterley, fetch a load of coal which'd be five hundredweight them days, course it was hard on a ruddy horse, I tell you........then he'd deliver that coal around the hills, five hundredweight a time and it was sixpence a hundredweight to lug it.   Gordon Cook

Options for children leaving school at fourteen or earlier in South Shropshire were limited, though options were at least available. The move from school and home to the adult world of work was always an eventful one and could at times be traumatic and difficult.

Here, Johnny Butler, Johnny Roberts and Heber Rowson share their experiences of 'starting work'.

When I left school – I expect I was a liability – so I left school on the Friday and on the Monday morning mother took me up to put me out on a farm, up Hope valley at Venus Bank. Told me to behave myself. It was a queer old system, if I wanted to come home in the week I'd got to ask if I could go and I remember once coming home and mother was there, "What brings you here?, come and have a cup of tea and get you off back!" I was fourteen years of age.   Johnny Butler

After I left school I went to Snailbeach picking spar for Joe Roberts for twenty eight shillings a month. I stayed there about eighteeen months. Then I went to work at the Creamery after that. We used to get tuppence ha'penny an hour to start off with. It was terrible money. You'd be working at seven o'clock in the morning and you'd still be there at seven o'clock at night before you knocked off and there you'd be going to knock off when there'd be an order in for so many thousand tins of canned stuff and we'd be there till ten or eleven o'clock at night. Then you'd have to bike all the way back up to the Stiperstones and you still had your jobs to do when you got home. I was there about two to three years.   Johnny Roberts

I started work at The Green at fourteen, taking out papers first, and on the farm after. I got four bob a week and me meat (meals). I was there until I was sixteen. Then I went to the Creamery banding boxes of condensed milk for Woolworths. I got nineteen shillings and four pence a week. One morning I got behind. I'd got three or four boxes coming down the runway when owd Gurden, the boss, came. He said I was idle and summat, he played holy hell up with me, so I took him one under the clock! About ten minutes later I was on me bike with me cards in me pocket. You couldn't get on the council them days 'til you was twenty-

one, so I went to Lea Cross and I seen this surveyor and I said I was twenty-one the other month. I was only seventeen and he said I could start.

Heber Rowson

Wallace Evans began his working life in the offices of the Malehurst Barytes Crushing Mill. His responsibilities were many and varied.

When I left school I went to Malehurst as an office boy. I was one of a number who could never get the stamp book to balance. I was frequently sent to Pontesbury for insurance stamps and I had to pick up the boss's lunch. I used to go round the works and get the orders for fags. I used to go round all the work-shops scrounging. By that time I had started to smoke and they all had to give me one – I often ended up with a packet of ten. There was four in the office and the boss, a couple of chaps in the carpenter's shop, there was a blacksmith's shop.

There was two different grades of barytes. One was pure white and the other a fawny colour. It went away into the paint and rubber industry. They had their own railway siding there for sending the stuff away and lorries used to lug it. The barytes was coming from Huglith then, the old ropeway was going all day long. I used to go down to the end of the ropeway in my dinner hour where Cecil Mansell was tipping the buckets and have a go at tipping buckets, but there was an art to it. I remember the old man who used to look after the ropeway, Tom Heath from Worthen, he was on all weathers, up and down the line greasing, he was a very weathered old man.

It was quite a big industry and there were a lot of men down there. A lot of them were exempt during the war as well as the miners. Afterwards they built that new factory there for 'heavy water', I think they called it. It was very hush hush. There weren't many working there. They had three shifts and there were vats bubbling.

I left Malehurst to come home and help my dad on the farm. He had silicosis, he worked at the Bog, Huglith and south Wales in the coal mines. My dad said he always used a muffler round his mouth and it must have helped him a lot because he was sixty-seven when he died when others died at a very young age.

Wallace Evans

Although 'flexible working patterns' were still a thing of the future, people would make a living in whatever way they could.

I always wanted to do hairdressing. My dad used to cut hair and he taught me. I cut hair for people for many years. Ivor Jones from Crowsnest played a trick on me while I was cutting hair up the Crowsnest one night. I left my little Bantam motor bike by his house and he greased the throttle so much I couldn't grip it. I got my own back – the next time he asked me to cut his hair I cut half of it and took his one eyebrow off and left!

Clifford Lewis

We were very poor but we had a good garden and father used to do a bit of gamekeeping for his cousin around the woods. His cousin owned the wood that stretched from Pontesbury right up to the top of Crowsnest Dingle. He would send a postcard and say what he wanted. Probably this week he might want so many rabbits and pheasants, then another week he might want so many posts and rails and things like that.

Elsie Rowson

The postal service played a vital role in everyday life. It also provided employment for many local people with a network of delivery routes covering the whole of the country and letters and parcels delivered on foot or bicycle day in, day out, even in the most extreme weather conditions. The post had to get through!

My Uncle Bert was mother's brother. He was wounded in the 1914-18 war he only had one leg, the other was an artificial limb. He'd leave Pennerley at half past three in the morning to go to Minsterley to sort all the letters for all those up Snailbeach, and up to The Bog and all up to Hope and the Gravels. The round was recognised as a walking postman's job but he did have a cycle which wasn't really permitted! Mail always got delivered on Christmas Day the only day they had off in the year was Boxing Day. He would travel from Minsterley all the way back up to The Bog delivering the mail, he would go home to Pennerley and then he would have to go back down at night collecting all the mail from the boxes to take it back to Minsterley. He would travel during the winter months through the snow. He would get a broom and tie a piece of cloth around it to have under his arm to help him through the snow.

Graham France

The postman's hut at The Bog was where he used to have his sandwiches and sell stamps. He'd take the letters in and used to start back to Minsterley at 4 o'clock collecting the letters all the way down. It was a galvanised hut and he had a little stove in there to boil his kettle. He had an artificial leg.

Millie Gough

Dora that lived at Ritton Castle used to have a lot of catalogues and Uncle Bert used to be mad because she'd order these corsets and he'd say, "I've got to go all the way to Ritton Castle with this parcel and probably it wunna fit and I shall have to take it back."

Doreen Rowson

Uncle Bert at his post-hut at the Bog.

On Saturdays I used to help him with this mail. I'd go along the lane at Pennerley, he'd give me 6d and sometimes I used to go in the summer holidays to help him.

At the end of the lane was a Mr and Mrs Smout and they had a smallholding and she used to swear! This particular day there was one of these returns like an Agricultural Return, well my Uncle Bert filled all these forms in for them, all the way up through Snailbeach and Stiperstones, if there was any form filling in – they used to get him to do it because he was pretty well educated. This particular form he would have done for Mrs Smout – well she was swearing 'cos this form had come and she was just lighting a fire. She threw this form at me. I'd be pulling her leg and having a joke with her – I threw it back at her because she threw it at me and it landed in the fire! Of course she was worried – so was I! It was a Ministry form so she had to see my Uncle Bert and he had to send away for another form for her – so I lost my job for misbehaving!

Graham France

Mum had the Snailbeach Post Office for twenty-five years after gran who had also had it for twenty-five years before that. All through the war gran ran the post office and mum did the post round. She was the post woman.

They would read letters to an awful lot of people that couldn't read and they would write letters back for them. Mum used to spend a lot of time doing this, like, when she got up to Abel Bennett's, poor old Abel couldn't read nor could his wife, so she had to read anything they got and reply to it for them if they needed it.

At the post office basically it was just ordinary stamps and letters, there were a few pensions but not an awful lot and a few parcels. Telegrams were delivered from Minsterley, somebody on a bike would bring them.

Her round was a long way. First of all in the morning she would go down Lower Work, then all the Upper Works. From Upper Works to Lordshill, to the Vessons, over to the Hollies, up to Blakemoor Flat then right over the back of the hill and back down Perkins Beach Dingle, finish the Dingles and walk back home. You did it the opposite way round the next day, so they got their letters early. Everyday she would do it. One day when it snowed like the clappers she came across Mytton Dingle. There's a sheep track right across the very top before you tip down into the Ventor Dingle and it was all ice and she slipped down and she was wearing corsets, the old-fashioned corsets with steel ribs in them. She froze to 'em and she was up there hours.

When I wasn't at school I automatically went with mum. But my poor old dog used to go every day for a walk. He was a sheep dog. When we got to the Vessons, Mr Corfield farmed it then, we used to have a piece of pie and a cup of tea while he used the sheep dog to fetch the cows in. Then we'd get right over to Aunty Em's and have another piece of pie and a cup of tea. It were a long walk.

Phyllis Jones

The post round was eleven miles and six furlongs. That's if you did the lot. I can remember what I did with the money, I bought a tilley lamp and a mangle because I had Pat a baby, and I hadn't got a mangle. You were wringing all the washing out by hand otherwise. But what I remember most about the round was the loads I carried. You could see advertisments in the paper for big batteries, if you sent for two you got quite a discount. There was no electric in this area at all then. So they used to get together and send for two and I'd have those to carry. They'd weigh about ten pounds each and you'd carry those right to Gittinshaye and by the time you got there it would be pulling your neck out.

Elsie Rowson

Whilst at the Gravels Post Office:

A brace of pheasants would have a label round their necks with a stamp on. A rabbit would have a bit of wrapping round the middle with the address on. The odd pigeon perhaps, but it was usually a brace of pheasants they'd be sending off from here to their relations in the towns.

Jim Booth

Going 'into service' was one of the main opportunities available to girls (and some boys) leaving school in the first half of the 20th century. It was certainly not an easy option, however, with long hours and hard manual work very much the order of the day.

I was fourteen when I left school. I went out into service down to Minsterley to Rose Bank, it was Pemberton's then and he was the boss at the creamery. They had a little boy. On a Thursday I had a half day and used to walk up to the Crowsnest home.

Lydia Harrison

I left school at fourteen and went into domestic service for five shilling a week. I would have one half day a week off and a day every other weekend. My first place was for Mr Gray, manager of the mine at Snailbeach. I went to them first at Hanwood and then Pennerley House. I would look after the children and do the housework. After that I went to Captain Shepherd's at Oak House Minsterley where I was a parlour maid and waited on the table. There was a cook and a boot boy there.

Sarah Ann Evans

I went out to work when I was fourteen on a little farm. I did the milking and feeding and everything. Then after that I got into Linley Hall but before that I went up to London for six months. A person from Lydbury North wanted somebody to go and work for her. So I went with her and two other girls from around there and we went up to London for six months. It was lovely.

Nora Pinches

When I left school I was working on the surface at Snailbeach and I wanted to go to Huglith. I was only getting eight bob at Snailbeach when them at Huglith was getting twenty-four bob. Anyway, my mum said she'd get me a job, and she did, at Wollas Hall, Pershore in service. Harvey Mountford, from the Frogs Gutter, his mother said the same thing and he ended up in Malvern. Wollas Hall was a big estate belonging to the Whitworth family and there were nine staff. I thought this isn't my type of work – it was the hardest job I ever had. I was waiting on tables, cleaning silver and cleaning shoes. If there was a shooting party I would have to clean twenty pairs of shoes and have them outside the doors by eight o'clock in the morning. We was on the go all the time. The kitchen maid was from Ross-on-Wye and the scullery maid was from Neath in South Wales and those little owd wenches were far worse off than me. Their hands would be chapped raw from peeling potatoes.

I wanted to run away but mum said I'd got to stick it. I was graded up to footman but after two years I came back to Bergam Mine and fifteen bob a week. I got married at nineteen and was in the Royal Navy as a gunner in the Atlantic when I was nineteen and a half.

Clifford Lewis

The Second World War affected people's lives in many different ways. For Millie Gough, it led to her having a rare opportunity to see how the other half lived.

I worked outside with dad on the farm, milking, driving the tractor, driving the horses, everything that had got to be done, we did. No sooner than I left school the war came and one brother went in the army and the other decided to leave, so it left dad and me to run the farm, otherwise I would have to have gone in munitions or something like that. I worked on the farm for about four years until I went to work at Bishops Castle, mum said I better go and see how the other half of the community lived. I went to Tudors, the cafe, in Bishops Castle and I had to do a bit of everything, wait on tables, cleaning, ironing, prepare the vegetables and do the cooking. They had boarders in there. I worked there for about two years and then I went to work for Mr Pugh, the tailor. That was in his private house, he was ever so good to me – he made me all sorts of clothes. I was sure to be the best dressed person in the Bog while I worked there. Everything was done to a timetable and you did everything that had to be done in the house.

Millie Gough

The Second World War was to bring about a great change in the lives of women and in their occupations.

I worked all through the war. At the commencement of the war I was working nights at the Creamery for three pence ha'penny an hour and I said to Miss East, who was Mr Gurden's secretary, "I've had enough of this, can I see Mr Gurden please?" And she said, "I'll see if I can get in touch". She did and he gave me a farthing an hour rise, working nights from seven o'clock at night to seven o'clock in the morning and then biking home. After that we were transferred to the factory making stew for the soldiers, the meat would be frozen. It was terrible cold there at the factory. Then I got a job at the shop at Minsterley and was there for the rest of the war.

Mollie Rowson

During 1944-45 my dad was foreman over a small band of men that felled the Nipstone Wood. They tushed that out with heavy horses. It took 18 months to 2 years to clear it right down to the road at Frogs Gutter.

The women would saw the wood up for between a ha'penny, three farthings a pit prop. The majority went to the pits. The women did the sawing by hand and the peeling with an old peeling iron – a most peculiar tool.

Henry Jones

There were a lot of people employed, there would be women digging the docks from corn, women potato picking. One farm I worked at would send a cattle wagon to bring a load of women to work. We referred to them always as 'the women'. One man said to me once, "I expect you're busy potato picking". "Oh no", I said " 'the women' do that!" I got a very funny look. I was hefty and I helped load the bags of potatoes, 'the women' filled!

Horses were lovely to work with. I loved the work with horses. A horse splitting a furrow to set potatoes will walk very neatly on top of the furrow. The plough cuts it through and tips the soil onto the two furrows with the potatoes in. You set potatoes by having a bag tied round your neck and you dropped them in one by one. Every time you put your foot down, you put a potato down.

Connie Read

In the years between the Wars, the general economic depression hit home in the remote rural areas of South Shropshire as much as it did anywhere else. A special 'dole' office was set up in Gornall's Hut, Station Road, Minsterley.

The dole office was in Minsterley and there'd be a gang of blokes from there to the creamery. They went down there twice a week. Once to sign on and the next to draw their two or three shillings, like – whatever it was. But if they'd got stock, like an old cow or anything, well then there was the means test and if you'd got anything then they'd dock so much off your dole money – it was a poor old existence. And for some of them they only got as far as the Bath Arms or the Bridge or the Miner's Arms as they called it in those days so there was very little ever went home and it was hard going.

Johnny Butler

You could draw unemployment benefit if you put so many hours work in, whoever you worked for had to sign a slip to prove that you worked for them. In Minsterley they signed on at a place called Gornall's Hut. I remember getting in a queue there with the men, I'd just gone down to see if there was any work they could fix me up with. The unemployment people used to come out from Shrewsbury to pay the men.

My grandfather Thomas was something to do with unemployment. He used to pay out unemployment money and to save the men going all the way to Bishops Castle to collect their money he would take the money up to The Bog and pay it out there. The Bog was a ramshackle place, sheds and tin roofs and mine workings, the miners' welfare and the school.

John Francis

Life was hard in the late nineteenth and early twentieth centuries. People gravitated to wherever work was to be found, including the Snailbeach lead mining area. At one time approximately five hundred men were employed at Snailbeach.

Emily Griffiths

Clifford Lewis came from a family who had been involved in the Stiperstones mining industry for a number of generations. His forebears had experience at first hand of the ever present risk which a miner's life entailed.

I lost two great grandfathers and almost lost my grandfather in two separate mining accidents at Snailbeach. In the 1860s my maternal great grandfather Samuel Edwards began work at the Snailbeach mines where he became a pitman, but while inspecting the Engine Shaft in 1875 the timber gave way and he fell down the mine and was killed. He left behind his wife, a sixteen year old son Thomas, who was already working at the mine and five daughters. Thomas, my grandfather, was given a man's wage to raise the family as recompense for his father's death.

My paternal great grandfather was also to meet his death at Snailbeach, George Lewis was one of seven men who plunged to their deaths when the rope supporting the cage they were travelling in broke on March 6 1895. His son,

William Lewis, was also in the cage but at the last minute stepped out to fetch some tools and another miner took his place. William Lewis was my grandfather. My grandparents would never allow my father to work underground so he worked on the surface of the Snailbeach mine on the Buddles [ore dressing]. Bearing this in mind, in 1937, at the age of fourteen, I started working underground for Tom Evans and Jack (Gorsty) Lewis at The Knolls Mine, Cold Hill where I picked and stacked deads [pieces of rock] for eight bob a week.

Clifford Lewis

Records reveal a total of 33 fatal accidents in the South Shropshire 'metalliferous mining area' from 1875 onwards. The plain statistics, however, do not reveal the dreadful impact that such tragic deaths must have had.

My father owned Weston Mine (Cliffdale) at Priest Weston. It was a big barytes mine with a hundred and eighty men working there at one time. It was running at the same time as Snailbeach but carried on running until 1936 when my father closed the mine. We had another one, Roundton, two lads got killed there, Oliver Davies and Ern Whitall, they were from the village of Priest Weston. One was burnt to death and the other died in a rock fall. My father was very religious. We closed everything down on a Sunday.

Ken Lewis

GEORGE'S SHAFT.   SNAILBEACH MINE 1965

There were of course many scientific and technical ways of establishing the presence of barytes and other minerals in the ground. Some local men, however, had a particular gift for doing it their own way.

At the turn of the century you could start anywhere. In that day and age they used to go plundering – my grandad and all them old miners. They would have a clock spring or a hazel stick and they would be divining to find water or barytes. The stick would come over, you canna hold it – it dunna work for everybody.

Heber Rowson

I tried my hand at divining for barytes, it's something similar to divining for water but you use a clock spring instead. We tried it up the Lordshill Bank where the barytes was

showing in the ditch at the side of the road. It seemed to work for me!

Clifford Lewis

Compared to most of the other job opportunities available to men from the Stiperstones area, mining was relatively well paid. When local mining ventures began to close, many preferred to seek similar work far away from home – with all that this entailed in terms of travelling and leaving their families – to the limited alternatives available to them in Shropshire.

My old grandfather, the old John Butler, was the gamekeeper and while he was at it father worked at the Bog in the lead mines. When he died, our father did it. But Huglith was opening up and the money was better so he went mining – barytes mining. Mining fluctuated and at one stage father went mining anthracite in South Wales.

Johnny Butler

Grandad worked at Snailbeach, Tankerville and The Bog but to finish up he worked in the South Wales collieries. When the lead mine at Snailbeach finished (1911) many of them would travel from The Bog to New Tredegar and Old Tredegar collieries [near Merthyr Tydfil] in South Wales. There was nothing else for it in that day and age. There was no dole or anything and no money.

Heber Rowson

My gran was left to work on the farm and grandad went to work in South Wales to the coal pits. They had eleven kids.

Jim Harper

When the mines closed at The Bog my grandad and a lot of others went to work at the Rhayader dams. They would set out on a Sunday afternoon to get there in time for the Monday morning shift walking most of the way.

John Bennett

Emily Griffiths' prodigious memory and knowledge of local mining lore was legendary. Here, she provides a detailed description of the clothing worn by Stiperstones miners – amongst whom were many members of her family.

For work a miner wore an undershirt and long johns, a flannel or union (mixture of flannel and cotton) shirt with a collar stud, corduroy or moleskin trousers. These would be hitched below the knee with a piece of string called 'yorks'.

Stockings were black and home knitted with knitted garter stitch garters which went round twice below the knee and the end tucked in. Hob nailed boots with a laced over tongue (a solid tongue with no space up the sides), which were laced with real leather strip laces. These boots would be greased with goose or hen fat every night to make them waterproof. Inside his boots and stockings, the careful miner bound his toes with old rags much as a boxer's fingers are bound inside his gloves. Hence the saying that an untidy, ragged person was 'a proper owd toe rag'! Any old jacket passed wearing for best, uniform tunics, even swallow tail coats could serve for work. To crown all was a bowler hat (the curly brimmed type), hardened with resin and holding a lump of clay with a tallow candle enfixed.

Emily Griffiths

In the winter time the miners would get up and go to work before it got light, they'd work underground in candlelight and come home in the dark. They never saw daylight.   John Bennett

By the First World War all major work at Snailbeach mines had ceased with the exception of Perkins Level and the reworking of the spoil heaps. Between 1937 and 1938 Tom Evans and Jack 'Gorsty' Lewis acquired a lease to work a part of the Snailbeach mine known as Paraffin Level. This was a relatively small concern with about eight to ten men working on average an eight hour day.

Jack 'Gorsty' Lewis was the boss and Johnny Williams was the foreman. Tom 'Boss' Evans handled the transport. One of my responsibilities was to keep the mine free of water using a rotary pump. Drilling was done by hand and gelignite, not powder, was used. The gelignite was kept in the magazine house at Buxton near the Tankerville mine and Jack Corfield had the key. Nobel produced the gelignite and it came by van from Penrhyndaedryth (Wrexham). As I had to pass Buxton on my way to work, I collected the gelignite from Jack Corfield. I had a push bike then and I carried the gelignite, detonators and fuses all together in a bag on my shoulder. It was madness, I was only fourteen!

Clifford Lewis

My father was a custodian of the old magazine at Tankerville, farmers would use gelignite to blow up tree roots. The magazine was licensed by the Home Office, the police had no jurisdiction. During the Second World War it was full of gelignite and explosives for Gresford Colliery, near Wrexham. Very often I had to go and fetch ten pounds of gelignite, tuck it inside my coat and go off on my bike with it. It was only dangerous if it was damp. The detonators were kept in a separate place. There was a steel sheeted door, then three lots of doors. No matches or cigarettes were allowed and everything had to be brass so there were no sparks.

Emily Griffiths

Most of the miners had dynamite, fuses and caps stored away on the top of the grandfather clock. If they wanted to

Young Barytes miners of the 1930's.
Back row: foreman Mr Will Hughes, Billy Pinches, George Adams, Peter Pugh, Joe Rowson, Bob Downes.
Front row: Tom Lewis, Tom Jones, Eric Davies.

Tankerville Lead Mine 1980

*blast a tree root up or any other job requiring explosives
they just did it.* From "Recalling the Past" by George Evans

Within six months of Clifford Lewis starting work at Paraffin Level there was an event which put the wind up him and Heber Rowson too:

The nearest I ever came to death was when I worked for Jack Lewis and Tom Evans. It was afore I went to Huglith and we was working up the Paraffin Level at Snailbeach and we got a great big bed of barytes there. We was getting a lorry load a day out – drilling it and clearing it out. We was having our lunch one morning and we heard one hell of a roar and a bang. When we went back from our lunch the lot had gone. The turn tree, the shovels and everything all to the bottom of Snailbeach – we might have all gone with it! I tell you what, the Lord was with us that morning. Heber Rowson

Snailbeach mine was unique locally in having its own narrow gauge railway running from the mine site down to join the Minsterley branch line at Pontesbury. Its primary purpose, at least in the early days, was to carry mineral away from the mine and bring coal and other supplies up to it.

Gordon Cook, however, remembers that for him and his work mates 'picking spar' on the extensive Snailbeach spoil heaps, the railway brought a more welcome cargo each month.

Then there was Snailbeach mines. I worked there a bit. They used to pay 'em out once a month, the wages. Used to bring it up from Pontesbury Station on the little train up to Snailbeach.

There was a carriage especially for the bloke to come up on and they used to bring the wages up once a month. They would pay us out there. I used to get two pounds one month and one pound ten shillings another for picking spar, fifty shillings a ton. Gordon Cook

Some small scale local mining ventures, such as the Bergam Mine, South of Stiperstones village, survived the closure of the larger mines and in the case of Bergam was still operating during and after the Second World War.

The Locomotive shed at Snailbeach.

Clifford Lewis remembers happy days working there between 1940 and 1943 and Henry Jones remembers watching the mine workings in Perkins Beach as a boy.

In 1940 work was hard to find, so I went to work at Bergam Mine, I was seventeen. Edgar Evans was the foreman, Wilson Morgan and Tom Rowson were drillers. Tom Smith and Freddie Hotchkiss were barrowing and lashing back [shovelling barytes into an ore shoot] and Sam Purslow and George Evans worked the jigging tub [spar separator] . My job was tramming, bringing the barytes along a level to the surface. This was hard work and my back was often bruised from lifting the tubs. Once outside I emptied the tub and from there Jack Evans took over. His job was to fill a sledge up with barytes and then guide the horse and sledge down the hill to where it was loaded and taken by lorry to Malehurst. These were happy days for me, we worked two shifts, the night shift would drill and blast, and the day shift would clear out. It was here I had my first experience hand drilling. Usually there were three of us involved in the drilling, two strikers and one turning the drill. It was a lovely sound. All our work was done by candlelight. We bought the candles from Mattie Ridge's shop at the Tankerville. It was surprising how your eyes got used to the darkness underground. When they cut out the cranches (underground wooden supports) from the Tankerville mine we used the timber. We would come outside to have our bait in a little old cottage with a fireplace. Many a happy time we spent listening to Edgar Evans talking about Wales. In 1943 the work at Bergam became slack so I volunteered for the Navy.

Clifford Lewis

The spar works on the south side of Perkins Beach Dingle were on the really steep incline where the mining was in them days – only a small mine on the side. They used to lug the stuff down with a horse at the Ventor and store it there, sort it and then it was lugged away in the lorry when there was a load.

There was an old shire horse called Jack. He used to lug it down in what was called a 'car' and that was a big strong wooden box on two steel runners and he used to pull it down the bank with chains and it would just slip fairly easily behind him. He would have to tush the empty box up all the way. It was really hard tushing it up – like he'd walk forty yards and he'd stop and pant, he'd walk another forty yards and stop and have a puff. A fella called Jack Evans owned this horse. He farmed at The Green Farm near the school and us kids was always fascinated to watch him with this horse up and down the track they had worn in the hill over the time they were operating there, I should think some three to four feet deep continuously dragging the car up and down.

Henry Jones

They took a lot of stone out of the hillsides

They took a lot of stone out of the hillsides, thousands of tons from Tankerville went to Shawbury, Sleap and Cosford aerodromes. For a couple of years there was a team of men with sledge hammers breaking the granite stone with 14lb sledges to about six inches in size. They worked all along The Devil's Chair and Cranberry rock all along the ridge. It took a year or two. A firm from Snailbeach with four or five lorries took two loads a day all loaded by hand to the airfields. Thousands of tons came from Shepherd's Rock and went down the Lordshill. The first bed of each runway was six inch stone.

Henry Jones

My father had a horse and an old sledge, 'cars' we used to call them. They would be filled up and brought down to where The Devil's Chair car park is now. Men would break the stone with sledges and a horse and cart would lug it out on to The Bog road. It was used to make The Bog road and the school yard at The Bog school. The stone would take some breaking. They had four or five sledges and the 'knappers' (head of a hammer) were not very big. Finding the grain was the art of it.

Les Hotchkiss

At the Nipstone there was a little tram that brought stone to the side of the road. Reg Williams lugged the stone with a solid wheeled little lorry, there was no cab on it but they did make one. My father was out of work and he went up to the Nipstone moving stone. It was hard work and it would make them sweat the pig fat out of 'em! The Stiperstones rocks are pretty hard but if they found a good vein it would be easier.

Henry Owen

From the yard at the mine came weird, plaintive sounds, as the rock crusher ground the body of the mountain to fragments. These sounds were so wild and eerie that they might have been the forlorn music of fairy players sitting shadowy and huge, in the dim rock foundations, fiddling madly of nameless terror, fluting of unreachable beauties and rocky immortalities, harping on their own heartstrings to the deaf heartstrings of men. Deborah listened and thought of Stephen down there, with his shirt sleeves rolled up, his *nostrils a little expanded with excitement in the giant work he controlled, his nod bringing a fresh trolleyful of rock to be ground up.*

From The Golden Arrow by Mary Webb

Stonecutters at Snailbeach

Gangs of men came from the mines, the mining was running out in the Stiperstones area, Huglith and The Bog. We [T.O. Tomlins, Halfway House] were finding them work, there'd be eight or ten in a gang. They used to sit straight-faced in the lorry that fetched them, never blinked an eye or smiled in any shape or form, but my word they'd work, they were splendid men and you could trust them.

They had to meet the lorry at seven up at the Stiperstones and they'd ALWAYS be in the lorry at seven, not getting in it, not queueing to get in it, no they'd be sitting in the lorry at seven o'clock. They would get here at twenty-five past seven on the dot.

Ethel Tomlins

The Shrewsbury coalfield covered a considerable area south of the county town. In the 18th and 19th centuries, coal was being mined close to the Stiperstones, at villages like Asterley and Pontesford. The Hanwood colliery was at one time a large undertaking. In the two decades before the last war, it was producing 25,000 tons of coal a year and in the early 1920s employed nearly two hundred and fifty men.

Harold Hartshorn remembers going underground at Hanwood at the age of fourteen.

I left school on the Friday at fourteen and dad had got me down Hanwood Colliery on the Monday, still fourteen!

When the Second World War started, I was a Bevan Boy, they wouldn't take me in the army 'cos I was a miner.

Hanwood Colliery was very hard. The men that got the coal were working in spaces only eighteen inches high and they were lying on their shoulders with a pick cutting the coal out all day long for eight hours a day. I was one of the boys........

they'd fill a little sledge thing and you'd have a rope around your waist and a chain going through your legs, you'd hook into this sledge and drag it to where they filled the trucks on your hands and knees and then take it onto the main lines all underground. My first week's pay was fourteen shillings and nine pence, my dad was getting thirty-two shillings a week as a coal getter. Coal mines were better to work in than lead mines, conditions weren't very good but you weren't so likely to get a disease as you could in the lead mines.

You'd get 'black damp' (methane gas) in the coal mines, you wouldn't be able to breathe and they wouldn't let you go down. The fireman would always go down first with a lamp, and if his wick went down then it was dangerous and you couldn't go down until the 'black damp' had cleared.

They used to bring ponies down in the cage and they'd sit down on their behinds as they loosed them down. They always had ponies down Hanwood mines to pull the trucks.

Harold Hartshorn

As lead mining in Shropshire drew to a close, the mines in the district were forced to seek alternative mineral production to prevent closure. When Snailbeach mine closed in 1911, Huglith had already established itself as a highly productive barytes mine. Commencing production in 1910, it reached its peak in the mid 1930s exceeding twenty thousand tons per annum, employing sixty-five men. It closed in 1947, having produced over 290,000 tons of barytes.

Once extracted, the barytes was crushed and purified, a process known as 'ore dressing', and used in the paper, paint, rubber and chemical industries. An aerial ropeway, similar to the one which had earlier run from the Bog mine, took the barytes over Pontesbury Hill to the Malehurst mill.

My father, Charles Pidwell, was a mining engineer and he worked at South Crofty mine near Cambourne in Cornwall. A lot of Cornish miners went all over the world mining. My father was in South Africa mining when the First World War was declared, he immediately came back to volunteer.

When he came out of the army he must have applied for the job at Huglith. Colonel Ramsden was one of the people involved in putting money into Huglith in those days, he was one of the directors of the Shropshire Mines Company which operated The Bog, Pennerley, Huglith and various levels round about. My father was involved in the opening up of the mine at Huglith. We came to live at Little Minsterley for a few months, then to The Hollies in Station Terrace and then the White House, Little Minsterley.

Huglith Mine was in the trees, and the old engine house. Further on they built a bungalow for the engine driver, George Betton. The offices for the mine were at Malehurst.

For a time they would bring barytes down to the sidings at Pontesbury on big dreys pulled by four horses. Pugh's, The Vessons had that contract and they had all these lovely shire horses they were up and down each day. Long flat wagons with all this stuff piled on. Some horses were bigger than others. Pughs used to lead the horses, there were lots of sons, there was Jim and Roy and others. When the aerial ropeway was built the horses stopped. That ropeway was a work of art.

I remember one winter, father had a big leather bag with a strap over his shoulder and on a Friday morning he carried the wages. I expect in good weather he would have been taken with the money but it was a frightful snow storm so he carried the bag, a lot of the way he was walking on top of the hedges. The snow was level with them and rather than the men not have their wages he walked all the way with the cash. He was quite exhausted when he got back. My father left Huglith at the end of 1934 after being there fifteen years. He retired and moved back to Cornwall to his roots leaving my brother who had served his apprenticeship at Malehurst and was then working at Huglith looking after engines and machinery.

Eileen Higley

Jim Harper and Heber Rowson both went to work at Huglith after leaving school.

When you were fourteen you had to leave school, there was only the mines or farming as an option there was nothing else.

You'd got to be sixteen before you went underground. I never went underground until I was old enough, so I worked on the top helping two men to tip barytes out of the tubs, clean them out and put them back on the ropeway to go back underground. I had to be there at seven o'clock and I finished at four. It was a pound a week but when you went underground it was two pound. We was living at the Stiperstones at the time and we walked up over the hill, there'd be four or five of us go together – we'd meet Heber up by the Devils Chair, we'd shout him, like.

Jim Harper

Do I remember my first day at Huglith? How could I ever forget it. Little did I know what was in store for me when I went below. The miners had a sort of initiation ceremony which was kept a great secret from all newcomers. My first inkling of this came as I was grabbed and pinned down by four or five miners. I couldn't budge I yelled and struggled to loosen myself, my yells soon turned to screams when I realised that they was removing my trousers. Someone brought a bucket of black grease that they used for the tram wheels. Well they got that grease...............

Heber Rowson

The rough humour involved in such initiation ceremonies extended to other aspects of the miners' lives together – including their meal times.

My first job was 'lashing back' this mainly involved shovelling barytes into an ore chute, then the trams would come underneath to load up. I did this for two years and worked from seven until three with only one break of half an hour for lunch. We were very thankful for this break especially the older miners who were worn out from this hard physical work. Times were hard, you could always have done with a bit more to eat. Still we always had time for a joke or a prank or two. Most people in those days had small holdings and kept a few pigs and cattle. Whenever one of the lads killed a pig you always knew he'd have a nice meat pie in his bait box. The person with the pie was the envy of us all, and he knew if he wanted that pie for his dinner he would have to hide his bait box good and proper! I remember on one occasion one of the lads let on to another that he had killed a pig and his wife had made him a pie. At dinner time he sat down to eat his pie but that other lad snatched it out of his hand and took a great mouthful, he had a smirk on his face as he started to chew, but the grins on the other miners faces and the taste of the pie soon told him something was amiss. Instead of pork, the pie had been filled with a concoction of cow dung and other unmentionable ingredients!

Heber Rowson

At any mine, there was a range of jobs to be done, both above and below ground. The jobs of time keeper and storeman were often combined and seemed to attract a particular type of person.

Arthur Woodman, a thin ex-military man stoked the boilers by hand and drove the winding gear. The miners worked 7am to 3.30pm – long enough in those days and in those conditions. The pay would be about three pounds ten shillings per week, and they would be wet through every day into the bargain.

Reggie Evans was the time keeper and the storeman. 'Little Reggie' they called him. He was a very straight-forward little chap. You would get what you were entitled to from Reggie but you would get nothing else. They would send me down to get a hacksaw blade and Reggie would say, "Well I think you had one last week!" but you always broke one or two when you were new, just starting.

Esmond Betton

When I went underground I pulled trams, some of them went for over one mile underground. I went driving the engine for a good while and putting the tubs in the cage. You'd got to be at work underground for seven o'clock. It would be no good going at one minute to seven or you could get back down the road! When owd Dunn was there, he reckoned nobody overlaid to a minute. If you overlaid, you overlaid! You wasn't turned away, you was sacked, that was the end of it, there was no messing! If you was poorly you wouldn't get paid anything.

You'd go and help on the farms in the evening or go rabbiting or go shooting, anything to get a bit of extra money for wine, women and song!

Jim Harper

Visits by the directors of the mine always brought with them the risk of a decision to cut jobs or even to close the mine. When it came, however, the chance to even the score a little could be a temptation too great to resist.

It was always a worrying day when Mr Reid paid a visit to Huglith, Mr Reid was a director, one of the head directors of the company at that time, a short, sharp, little chap, his eyes would look right through you. We were all a little afraid of him, if he saw you wandering about he would put his hand on your shoulder and he'd say, "Young man, you haven't lost much sweat today!" He would get out of his chauffeur driven Bentley, shake hands with Tommy Hawkins, have a good look round him and he'd say, "My word, Tom you've got far too many rabbits in your warren!" We knew what that meant, we knew all about that! We couldn't wait then for him to go to find out all the news, whether the mine was still going to carry on, or redundancies. It was all very worrying. I can see Tommy Hawkins walking up from his office. He'd come and break the news to us. Reprieved once again!

Esmond Betton

In trying to get more money for working in wet conditions ....

We peed on owd Reid. There was a big tank half way down the shaft for collecting water to pump it up onto the surface. We seed him coming down the cage, we got behind the tank and he never saw us. When the cage went past us, three of us peed on it. "It's not wet – it's just annoying!" said Reid, the silly beggar. Reid was the head man, like – he was the director of the mine. What he said was law.

Heber Rowson

The risks of sudden death and lingering illness were ever present. A chilling coincidence linked the deaths of three men who lost their lives at Huglith.

There were only three fatal accidents at Huglith. They were all on a Friday the thirteenth! When a thirteenth came on a Friday the old boss was always at the top of the shaft saying,

"You'll have to watch out today lads, it's the thirteenth, it's an unlucky day for you, remember". We were always very careful, like.
Heber Rowson

As I gained more experience in the mine I had the opportunity to go machining. This was the highest paid job for a miner but it was also the most dangerous job in the mine. Compressed air drills were in use to bore the shot holes. There was an increase in the levels of dust causing silicosis. My own father was to die prematurely at the age of 50 from silicosis. I refused to work in the stopes [underground caverns] on the drilling machines. The mine manager Tommy Hawkins then offered me a job tramming [pulling the trucks underground]. It was in 1939 for two pounds ten shillings a week.
Heber Rowson

Virtually everything used in the mine was made from either wood or metal and was manufactured 'on site'. The mine's carpenter and blacksmith played an essential role in its smooth running.

Albert Jones was the works carpenter. Albert suffered badly from arthritis and would get me to run errands for him. He would say, "Pop and fetch me a few nails, surrey, my poor owd legs are bad today". I always think of those words as I suffer from the same thing today. There was no surgery in them days, nor pain killers, they just had to get on with it! Albert's main job was to prepare the timber work when a new shaft was being sunk. This he would do in the week so it would be ready for the Sunday morning. That's when the job was mostly done. The timber for the shaft was made from about six by six square pine, in six foot sections and then held together by three-quarter round bolts about six inches long, threaded at both ends. This is what held the sections and what was mostly my job, and I had to get this ready for the Sunday as well.
Esmond Betton

Billy Lewis was the blacksmith and that was hard work. Sometimes it would mean using a sledgehammer all day, cutting three-quarters round iron to make ladder rungs. Billy's main job was to sharpen the drills for the miners and then to harden them in oil and water. There was quite an art to that job. The miners would bring them up the pit at half

past three and they would have to be ready for them the next morning. If they were not hardened properly, the underground foreman would have plenty to say.
Esmond Betton

Heber Rowson recalls working methods at Huglith mine in the last years before it closed when work was transferred to the nearby Sallies mine.

I went tramming with the lads. Every morning we'd get our lamps, a hard hat and our old clobber on. You'd take some carbine and water. To get to the shaft you had to get into a level thirty to forty feet, then there'd be the cage waiting for you at the top of the shaft. It went down at a 45 degree angle and took eight men at a time. There would be about three trips. You'd go in about ten to fifteen feet to the junction, you'd have a bit of a sing song and a bit of baccy. You could chew the bacca or smoke it. By God they never had the worms! I was about eighteen. I got six pounds five shillings a week but it was damned hard work.

After we all had our baccy some would go west and some would go to the east end and some would jump in the trucks. They'd go a mile up under old Huglith, what they call the North Cross. They had an endless rope running. At the top of the Cross turn right, go up the Mud Vein ever so far, all these owd wagons, twelve to fourteen wagons. Then you'd get out of the wagons and go to various places, stoping off the main level, a couple of hundred feet up, like.

All these old stopes would be full of barytes from the night shift, you had to fill all your wagons out of the hoppers, take 'em down to the top of the Mud Vein and hook 'em on the rope, press the bell and away they'd go, like. Then you had to follow 'em down to the bottom of the pit, push 'em into the cage one at a time and as one went up an empty one would come down. So you'd push that into a siding until you'd got another twelve to fourteen empty wagons.

They found this big bunch of barytes under Old Huglith – it saved Huglith for about five years and it was worked out. To finish up, there was nothing left there, so they decided then to sink down and went down another two hundred foot. They had a great big pump, a six inch pump in the bottom of there – there was some water there!

They drove out and stoped but never made a success of it. Huglith was about worked out. Then they sent us to the Sallies.

Heber Rowson

The Sallies barytes mine opened about 1937 and closed in 1948; during the later years nearly forty men were employed at this mine.

When Huglith Mine did eventually close, the rope wheel was still left there and working, to bring barytes from the Sallies Mine and Brownhills Mine to save taking it by road to Malehurst. There were three people involved, left behind to do the job. The chap on the ropeway was Will Evans from Lordshill Chapel cottage and with him was Ned Davies from Snailbeach. I was left there to help them out. I stayed with them for a while, then I went to the Sallies in the fitting shop.

Esmond Betton

By God there was some water there (The Sallies). Water right up to your knees!

Jim Harper

The work of an engineer at the mine was demanding, it was carried out by a skilled man. Even in the years up to the Second World War much of the work had still to be done by hand.

Bill Morgan was the engineer at the Sallies. He was a very good engineer, he could draw and he could do the job no problem to him. We used to watch Bill come up the road in his little Morris 8 car. He would get out in front of the office. If he stretched his arms out and his fingers out two or three times we knew Bill was in a bad mood. But apart from that he knew his job.

Bill drew the head gear for the Sallies and it was made in the mill at Malehurst. There was not much machinery in those days, and most of the steel work for the head gear was sawn by hand with a hacksaw! I think they had one machine but most of the work was done with hacksaws. Just to think about starting to cut through all that steel work with hacksaws would break your heart today, but they did it! It was built in one of the buildings at Malehurst and it was erected

before it was to taken to the site at the Sallies to see if everything fitted. And it did! It fitted like a glove. It was then transported from Malehurst to the Sallies. I think most of the steelwork was taken on the little old Morris lorry that belonged to the company.

Esmond Betton

Here Johnny Roberts remembers in detail work at the Sallies mine, the risks and the discomfort that inevitably went with it.

When I came out of the R A F I went to the Sallies [barytes mine]. It was terrible, you'd get underground and within ten minutes you'd be wet through. You were working in wet clothes all day. You'd start about seven and used to knock off at about half past three.

I was drilling – boring the holes. We used to go up what they called a level. You used to have a little owd mask over your face and we used to have what you call a dust trap. It was like a hose. It was put on the end of the drill and a lot of the dust went down the hose and into the dust trap.

You had the drill on your shoulder and bore two holes in the top, three in the middle and four in the bottom. You put what you called the cut holes at the bottom, they went in at an angle. The holes were about six foot – you used to blow it all out. You didn't get long out of the drills. You'd use them one day and send them the next to Malehurst to be sharpened. They had a blacksmith there.

Dynamite was put in the holes, they used to fetch that from Buxton out of the magazine. Jackie Corfield, Emily's dad [Emily Griffiths], used to bring it with a horse and cart. You used to get your dynamite and put one in first, then you'd get another....... put your fuse on, it had a little cap, press him down and then you'd ram him into the hole. Then you'd split your fuse and after you had charged all your holes you'd set your charge so that each fuse was a little bit longer.

I used to light it with a candle and you'd touch the fuse and you'd take like hell! You'd get the depth that you'd drilled and then you'd have to go in the next morning and work it all down with a pick. It was all solid, you'd get it all out and tram it out to the bottom and put it in the cage, and as one full one went up, an empty one came down.

Working underground at Sallies are: Wilson Morgan - drill, George WIlliams - vacuum pipe, Alf Lewis - bottom right, John Roberts - top right, Jim Harper - top left.

With two of you working and timbering, again you bored and charged your holes it was time to pack in. Sometimes you used to rise up, stope it and sometimes you would come to the grass roots.

1945-46 you'd get ten pounds a week working Monday to Friday, you didn't work very often on a Saturday. If you were poorly you just didn't get anything, not like you do today.

I don't remember when the Trade Unions started until I got onto the Post Office, and it was all Trade Unions there

Johnny Roberts

5: We plough the fields and scatter

As well as those who lived in the villages, many Stiperstones miners had small-holdings scattered over the surrounding hillsides. Their cottages had a number of acres of land and this allowed the families to supplement their income by producing much of their own food. One irate mine owner of the 19th century was led to remark that, because of the need to cultivate their own land, the miners were not entirely dependent upon their earnings at the mine for subsistence. This was apparently an undesirable trait as it made the miners too independent!

Such small-scale subsistence farming existed alongside a number of larger farms on the lower slopes of the Stiperstones. These also provided a useful source of employment for local men and women. The mines, of course, have come and gone but agriculture still provides the backbone of the local economy and community. People's lives still revolve to some extent around the seasons and the farming year. The huge Creamery at Minsterley may have turned its hand to the production of yoghurt, but memories of the days when its lorries trundled round the local lanes collecting churns of milk from wooden stands outside farm gates are still very fresh in local minds.

"Nobody had a garden just for flowers!"

Sarah Ann Evans (born 1911) came to live at the The Bog Mine cottages when she was six years old. Her father had contracted 'Black' Flu during the First World War. He had a job working on the surface of The Bog Mine. She remembers,

We had about an acre and a half that was put to hay to feed the animals in the winter. We had two cows for our own milk and butter. Any milk left over went into the washtub for the pig. Everybody had a washtub and all the waste went into it for the pig.

The dietary needs of the mining communities were very often supplemented by their small holdings, many of which had been in the family for many years.

In those days with these little holdings they had a field here and a field there scattered all about in different places. We milked a couple of cows, they were shorthorns.

Jack Pugh

Farming......it was a way of life, it was all a pleasure whatever you did. The big owd horses would tread on your feet – there'd be no tractors then. Land was more or less organic before the war. During the war they were forced to plough the ground and they didn't like it much. In the hay fields there would be dog dasies and rattleboxes. You could make a living off ten cows then.

Tom Pinches

We had a fourteen acre small holding and kept a cow, a pig and some hens. We used to milk, my mother made butter and sold it to the cottages where the miners lived because they had to buy a lot of things, but even they had a little garden of some description and grew their own vegetables, they would have a few hens scratching around. Nobody had a garden just for flowers. We grew potatoes in a patch on the hillside, half an acre just for potatoes. We had gooseberry trees, fruit bushes. We grew cabbages and carrots. We had to fetch our water from the well, but the water was never soiled even with cows around.

Margaret Buckley-Atkins

We might plough half an acre up to put six rows of potatoes and two or three rows of swedes and perhaps a turnip or two, might even be a little bit of vegetable, carrots, parsnips, if it was a little bit of favoured ground.

And there wasn't much favoured ground to be found at Pennerley where Henry Jones lived at number six.

Wallace Evans working the horses.

My grandfather used to set potatoes up Crowsnest Dingle up on the slope, I think the potato store is still there. My dad had a garden up above the reservoir (at Snailbeach) and as he was coming from Huglith he'd stop and garden and I can remember going up with mum to take his tea.

Mary Challinor

My granny lived next door on a little holding, she had got a little pony and trap and a couple of cows. We used to get the cows in for her. In the evening she used to say," Who's coming with me to 'farther' ? (fodder). Every evening about half past nine one of we children, if we were up we had to go with granny and she would put hay in front of the cow. And then back we would come with the lantern.

Mollie Rowson

Up at Pennerley Henry Jones recollects,

There was no straw – we'd never heard of soft straw round here. Fern (bracken) was the bedding. We cut fern with a scythe. Me dad used to cut fern every year and leave it to dry. We had a little pony and a little cart and he used to lug it in loose and store it in the building for litter for bedding. We had two cows and three to four calves at the most and thirty ewes.

We lived at the Apple Tree, a farm of about twenty acres. We kept cows, pigs and hens. I remember learning to milk by hand, there was no machines then. We had two pigs, they would have all the potato peelings and waste with meal added to it. One would be sold at market to pay for the feed. The other would be killed and kept for ourselves.

John Francis

It was also common for the miners and their families to keep more than one pig as Mrs Emily Griffiths remembers,

We would feed two pigs, one to eat and one to sell to be able to buy the salt to cure the other. Salt was so expensive.

Dad always used to give the cattle a bit of ivy on Christmas Day to eat. It is said that the cattle talk at midnight on Christmas Eve but I've never heard them.

Jack Pugh

Another superstition says that on Christmas Eve after a certain hour all cattle bow the knee in honour of Christ's birth in the stable. A tale is told of one curious person wishing to know if this was really so, and whose dead body was found with the cows the following morning.

Milking the cows was a twice daily chore to be accomplished, often as well as a 'day job'.

Dad worked in the building trade, he used to have to go to work but he had to milk before he went to Bishops Castle. I used to milk before I went to school, and then we used to come home from school and clean the cows out ready to bring them in to milk in the evening.

John Francis

Gilbert Hotchkiss milking at Welsh Row, The Bog.

Me dad used to milk six cows and go up in the morning and milk 'em and bring the milk down and carry it on two yokes to the Crowsnest to meet the milk cart going to the Creamery. He used to go up and milk at night and bring it down and put it in the cooler in the brook, stick the churn in the brook and some stones round it to keep it cool.

Gordon Cook

In 1947, the very bad winter, it froze the water and when you've got to carry the water to cows they seem to drink gallons. All the drinking bowls would freeze up in front of them. We didn't lose any animals but they did over at Darnford, they'd got no feed and the animals were eating the boards in front of them.

Betty Hordley

Although milking was a chore that was laborious and time consuming Bill Francis (John's father) very picturesquely describes the dairy he remembered from his childhood in his diaries published under the title *Hasty Pudding and Kettle Broth.*

During this summer weather and the loneliness of old age, one's thoughts revert to the days of one's childhood, remembering the good things and forgetting the bad. I see a long cool dairy with one or two barrels of home brewed beer on stands and a horn drinking cup upside down on

one. *A long shelf with shallow pans of milk, skimmed or waiting to be skimmed, a large dish of cold boiled potatoes to be taken at will when hungry, another of cold rice or bread pudding with stacks of raisins in it — also a hunger satisfier for young bellies. I had a thousand acres of mountain and moorland and field to wander in, with one rule only to be strictly observed (shut all gates after passing through), one hundred springs of pure water to satisfy a thirst and above all the pure air of heaven. One forgets the bad, or tries to. The lack of money – a penny was a fortune, the patched clothes, the darned socks and shoes with worn out soles. After all, one's neighbours were perhaps worse off. One forgets the midden in the yard and the smelly earth closet.*

Connie Read's memories as a Land Girl are of.....

a cow shed, a warm cosy place with wooden partitions which they called boskins. There were two cows in each stall chained up by the neck with a trough in front of them. They were up to their knees in lovely straw. In front of them was what they called the bing, a passage with bales of hay. You could walk along that and throw hay over to them. You sat on a three legged stool with a bucket between your knees and drew lovely warm milk into your buckets. It was a beautiful way of starting a winter morning. Your cow would be eating while you milked and then she would lie down and grunt with satisfaction having had a good breakfast. The milk was tipped through a sieve into a churn which stood outside the cowshed door. The cowsheds were in a square and in the middle was the mixen [the muck heap]. The lighting was by hurricane lamps. The first farm I worked on there were five of us milking but only four lamps, so if you were a bit late getting in, that was your hard luck. A boy would hold a candle while I rinsed the dairy things in a bath of cold water even when the snow was driving in. One farm had a pump outside the back door and a thousand pulls of the handle would fill the tank for the dairy. So I pumped a thousand pumps and there was still no water in the dairy! So I told the farmer and he went upstairs where there was PLENTY of water! There was a mouse in the pipe.

Connie Read

The miners' families and farmers' wives also worked hard.

I used to help with the milking before we had a milking machine. I was in and out of the house cooking meals and helping with the harvest or whatever. Sarah Ann Evans

Nora Pinches recalls her work in the dairy,

You'd strain it [the milk] and then put it to settle in big bowls and then take the cream off the top. We had a separator. It's funny how it separates the cream from the milk when the milk is warm, and we had that in big jars, great big jars, and when we got that full we had to churn it by hand in the big churn. It took some time sometimes, just according to the weather. If it was hot weather, it took a long time to come. It was all hard work in those days patting up the butter. We used to sell it to Challinor's at Pontesbury, what we didn't want.

We had a separator that you turned by hand that separated the cream from the milk; the cream was put into a big bowl to stand, and then mother would make butter using the old churn. You would have to turn it for about three quarters of an hour and then put the salt in and squeeze the water out. It would then be weighed out into one pound packs to be taken to Bishops Castle to be sold in the market.

John Francis

Churning day was once a week and any spare butter was bartered to the grocer for a bit off your bill. Sarah Ann Evans

Minsterley Creamery played an important role in the collection of the milk from the local farms and small holdings.

When I started at the Creamery first I had ninety six names on my book and you had to write them all a little ticket out. There were all these little farms that used to sell half a gallon in places, there was a woman at Pennerley, Mrs Brown, she only had one cow and when the cow went dry she would borrow some milk from Flossie Hughes so she could keep her licence for half a gallon.

I had a small lorry with forty eight churns on, you had to keep filling them up, if you had a gallon or half gallon you kept filling the churns up, they were marked on the inside and at every farm you had to measure the milk and write the

ticket out. The churns were left mostly on the side of the road.

When I picked milk up at Shelve I would take Wyke's children, Plant's children and Unwin's children to The Bog school. I had to take the little bottles of milk one third of a pint to The Bog school. There were thirty children there then.

Then I would pick up children for the Stiperstones school from Tomlins' and Williams', there were quite a few of them, and drop them off and fifty little bottles of milk. There was one little girl, Shirley Trow, we'd be going across The Bog road and she'd say, "Do sixty Les!", of course the owd arrow would fly round and we'd only be doing about thirty because it wasn't working right!

Les Hordley

Our milk went to Minsterley Creamery in churns in those days. In the summer time it was two pick ups a day, six o' clock in the morning 'cause the milk wouldn't keep. We started to milk at half past four and take it up to the stand at six to half past.

George Balmer

In the twenties, milk went to Minsterley Creamery, it was collected in a horse and cart or two horses and a dray. The Creamery supplied liquid milk to Birmingham. It went on the last train at 8 o'clock at night. It was called the milk train. It went in churns. They made cheese with the rest of the milk and later they made condensed milk in tins.

Jack Pugh

There was a market on the square at Minsterley where monthly cattle sales and an autumn sheep sale were held between 1879 and 1905, and a yearly Hiring Fair was recorded until 1937. Men and maids would be hired for the year. It was held on the bank in front of the Crown and Sceptre on each 3rd of May unless it fell on a Sunday.

Where the War Memorial now stands, pig and sheep pens were set up for the market each month during the second half of the 19th century.

From the "History of Minsterley" by Miss D T Merry

I remember selling sheep at the market at the War Memorial at Minsterley and then after the war down behind the Bath Arms in the yard.

They had hiring fairs at Bishops Castle, that was a big thing then the Bishops Castle fair. Lots of folks used to move once a year whether they'd got a good job or a bad one, they'd move on and they'd go to these hiring fairs to find a new job.

Jack Pugh

Sheep sale at Minsterley Square.

Whether it was just a few scraggy chickens around the garden or a hundred head of deep litter hens virtually every household kept poultry. Of course there were some superstitions about them.

If a hen is set on hatching eggs on a Friday the chicks will all be male.

A whistling woman and a crowing hen will fetch old Harry out of his den.

We'd keep chickens for eggs and mother would take them to Shrewsbury on the bus, on a Saturday to the market.

Jack Pugh

There was a hundred head of deep litter poulty, we used to rear chickens under brooders. Each week we would sell eight cases of eggs to Cheshire Farmers.

Farmers had geese. Smallholders wouldn't have them. Ten geese would eat as much grass as one cow.

Sarah Ann Evans

We
killed
about twenty
geese at Christmas.
There was more demand
for a goose. Turkey was a luxury in those days you couldn't
afford to eat one yourself unless you could rear one of the
damn things. They were very difficult to rear, very few
turkeys survived in those days. Between World War One and
World War Two you'd get a whopping great goose for ten
bob.

Jack Pugh

At a night time we had a big range coal fire and that fire was
always put to work either boiling pig potatoes, little rub-
bishy potatoes for the pigs in the morning or you'd get a
good armful of hay and put in this great big awd pot, pour
water on it and let it boil and boil all night. You'd keep pok-
ing it down with a poker and next morning when it had
cooled off put it in a bucket and feed it to the calves. We
called it hay tea. It was good stuff I tell you – it 'ud put a skin
on their backs.

Heber Rowson

We would keep the calves in a little shed behind their mothers and bring them out just for feeding so that we had the
milk just the same.

Margaret Buckley-Atkins

The prison farm was at Upper Vessons, it belonged to the
prison at Shrewsbury. My dad was the farm bailiff, he was
employed by the prison service and would instruct the prisoners in their duties. The prisoners would come out from
Shrewsbury on a lorry in the morning and go back at night.
The lorry in the meantime would take produce to other
prisons. We had sheep and some Welsh Black cattle and
two Suffolk Punch horses. I think they grew cabbages for
the prisons. Inmates I can remember included a doctor
and a gypsy who came back later to look after the horses.
Every one of them was very polite and gentlemanly. We
never had any worries about them. They were in prison for
petty crime or fraud and would usually be in the last three
months of their sentence. We had terrible fogs up there
and occasionally a prisoner would take the opportunity to
'get lost' but I can only remember a couple of actual
escapees. It didn't happen very often, there may have been
one or two who managed to stay out a night but they were
usually recaptured very quickly.

Kate Gittins

I remember the prisoner that escaped from the prison farm
and they caught him and took him to Mrs Owen, the shop,
and sat him on a chair. Mrs Owen said the prisoner was far
more civil than the warders!

Doug Boulter

On the first of May close your fields for hay

Harvesting was an important time of the year for the
whole community. It was a labour-intensive operation
before machinery had its impact on farming.

Hay was cut with a cutter pulled by one horse. It was raked
and then you went round and round with hay rakes and you
raked it into winrows and then you went round and round
with pikels and made it into haycocks, starting small and
going wider and wider at the top so the rain ran off it and in
due course that was tossed onto carts pulled by horses.
Then it was put into a stack and the stack would be thatched
or it could be put into a barn. It would be cut with a hay
knife – a big blade with a handle. You cut through the hay
and then you put the pikel in the piece you had cut and lift-
ed it. It was heavy – very heavy. Later on they got to bales
and now they have bales nobody can lift!

Connie Read

It was lovely in them days. It was all work though. I used to help in the hay – throw it up loose you know, and it'd be all down on me again.

Nora Pinches

We had cold tea while harvesting, but I couldn't bear cold tea. Oh no, oh God no. It'd go cold in the bottle, but if you was hot and thirsty it was all right .

George Balmer

Everybody helped one another when we were harvesting. Your neighbours would come and help you and you would help them. There were no tedders for us or anything like that we did it all with a pikel and a rake.

Sarah Ann Evans

We did it all with a pikel and a rake

The miners would earn some extra money by mowing for the local farm.

Grandad, Uncle Sam Williams and Uncle Fred Blakemore used to go mowing. They used to get up at daybreak and they'd mow until it was time to go to their shift at six o' clock at the mine. They'd go and do their shift and they'd go back and mow until dark. They couldn't bear that long field that goes down to the Hopyard, it was always known as the 'Wetty Meadow'. They couldn't bear starting on that, because as soon as ever they started on that it would rain, and of course in those days gathering the hay they wanted a dry time. They'd leave that 'til last if they could, because everybody was frightened of them starting the 'Wetty Meadow'.

Elsie Rowson

The men from the works would come and mow the hay fields, we carted it in on two poles at the Crowsnest, but we used horses at Lordshill.

Doris Hewitt

The men from the works would come and mow the hayfields: Joseph Rowson, Sam Williams and Fred Blakemore.

The harvest was wonderful, it was hard work though. It wouldn't be very early when we got the hay but sometimes I've known to be in the hayfield in August when it was Minsterley Show!

My dad had always got to clean the barn out 'cos we kids in the winter used to have a big rope in there and swing

Everybody helped one another when we were harvesting

once the hay was out. This swing would have to come down because he'd be getting ready for the hay. All underneath the hay used to be thorns to keep it off the bottom.

Mr Oldfield used to come with two horses. Granny wouldn't know when he was coming, then all of a sudden he'd come some evening and she'd have nothing in for him to drink and she'd make what she called "egg yot" She'd make a big jug of tea and beat eggs in it and milk, and it was nice. I'd take it up in the field to him and it would be getting dark, he'd sit under the hedge, getting dusk with these two horses, they'd been on all day tired to death, and me and him, all tired. He'd sit under the the hedge and he'd drink this and then he'd go home.

Well you'd be twisting and turning in this field for ages but then it was wonderful on the day when they started to lug it in. Just granny's little pony and a little flat cart. Granny had five sons and a son-in-law and they'd all be in the harvest field, they'd all have something to do.

We used to wait until dad came down with the pony and this little flat cart, we would wait at the barn because he would give us a ride back up to the field, then we would run all the way back to the barn! We would run up and play in the cocks of hay, you never see them today, cocks of hay,

things are different, they cut the hay in the morning and it's gone by afternoon now!

Mollie Rowson

They used rushes for thatching the haystack and fern for bedding the pig and tumping the potatoes. There was plenty of fern on the hills and heather stalks for the fire and moss for the wreath makers.

Doris Hewitt

We thatched the stacks with rushes, you'd get the longest rushes. It was a big owd job with string and pegs.

Wilfred Andrews

My grandfather went to Shrewsbury Show and he bought the first mowing machine that ever came up here, a one horse mowing machine it was called a Plannau, it was driven by a chain. It was in Rigmoreoak Patches for many years.

Les Hotchkiss

One wonders if it was these hay harvests that Mary Webb describes so vividly.

Sometimes it was September before the hay was safely carried; for it had to be done between storms, and storms were many. John cut it with a scythe, spare and tall in the clear purple morning. He would go up and down with vigorous movements, gravely followed by Rover; and a shadow man and a shadow dog went after them, dark and vast on the green field.

On the day it was ready to be lugged Joe came home early. A twill sheet on two poles reminiscent of an ambulance stretcher, was piled with hay and carried by Joe and John as carefully as if it really were an invalid.

But if rain clouds blew up as they generally did – the dignified march turned in to a mad rush; Rover protestingly exchanging his stroll for a trot, was half buried in falling hay; and as Mrs Arden said, "It was one pikel full for the rick and ten for the mixen." They all regarded lugging the hay as a game of hazard played against the forces of nature, and they played with spirit.

From "The Golden Arrow"

We always had a harvest supper when the hay was in – we were so pleased when the hay was in. Now granny would get her new potatoes out of the garden for that, and her peas, green peas, and she'd boil a piece of bacon and we had parsley sauce.

Two poles reminiscent of an ambulance stretcher were piled high with hay.

We kids would be dying to get in that house, we would be dying to get in for ours and we had to stay on the back yard until she had fed all the others. Oh that was hard; there'd be Aunty Sarah and Aunty Ruth and Aunty Lil all busy as could be getting the supper ready, and we'd have a lovely supper when we got in.

Then after that Aunty Ruth got on the organ and they'd sing all the old tunes.

Mollie Rowson

Opposite St Luke's Church on the edge of the village of Snailbeach lies the entrance to The Farm.

My parents kept Snailbeach Farm from 1902 until my father was killed in an accident in 1930. The lease to the farmhouse belonged to the mines, and the ground to Lord Bath. My grandfather had the lease on the ground until Lord Bath sold it, then he bought it. Mother and father moved into the farmhouse a month after they were married, when the mine's lease was up.

Living in the farmhouse at that time would be mother, father and eight children; there were two servants 'living in' and some of the workmen 'lived in'. Seasonal workmen slept in the bay in the hay. Dick and Sam Bailey came for hoeing. Mother used to feed them then they'd go back to the bay at night. One old man, George, he had big whiskers

and when I was little I used to sit on his knee, and I stuck burdock sticky balls in his whiskers when he was asleep, he grumbled! Mother had to cut them out with scissors! We had paying guests as well, Mr Attenborough, he was an estate agent, he stayed as a paying guest for quite a number of years. Gladys Groves 'lived in' as a servant, she met Dick who was the waggoner and they got married. Dad let them have one of the farm cottages and they lived there for many years and raised a family.

Della Pugh

When Johnny Butler's father died from the mining related disease, silicosis, his mother brought the family to The Farm Cottages to live.

The Farm in 1925 was a busy part of Snailbeach. Mr Percy Rowson [Della Pugh's father] was engaged in timber hauling. The timber from Crowsnest Dingle to Granham's Moor was being felled and horse-drawn timber carriages with four horses in a team was the norm. What a treat for young lads, hanging on the pole of the timber carriages until the waggonner flipped his whip round your bum!

Johnny Butler

The Farm in 1925 was a busy part of Snailbeach.

We had a lot of horses, my father was a timber haulier and he had the Snailbeach woods. The cart horses that lugged the timber carriages were 'Captain', then there was 'Blackbird', that was Tom Jones' favourite, and 'Topsy' but she was nasty, she had to be shod in a frame because she was so nasty, and there was 'Diamond.'

We used to go on the horses' backs up into the woods to collect brash and use it for heating the baker's oven. The horses would pull the bundles of brash back to the farm, this was called 'tushing'.

We had ponies as well, the white pony that pulled the trap was 'Nobby', mother had hand-reared him. When he was little he would come in the house, my grandma was alive then, but she was a bit senile, she'd say, "Take this old dog out!" Oh he was naughty, my brother used to have to corner him with the line prop, he'd bite!

Della Pugh

Both Tom Jones and his horse Blackbird featured in Johnny Butler's childhood.

On listening to Tom Jones drawing trees down the coppice with 'Blackbird' we learnt a few swear words. Then there was the excitement of watching Eddie shoeing 'Darling'. Why she was called 'Darling' heaven only knows, for she could kick a gnat's eye out. They had to put her in stocks to shoe her.

Johnny Butler

What I liked best of all on the farm was the lambs, I always had cade (hand reared) lambs on the bottle. One year I had three Betty, Billy and Mary. Johnny Butler and I would spend hours feeding these lambs. One died and we fetched bits of white spar to put around its little grave. That was Mary. Billy had to go to Mr Ellis, the butcher in Minsterley to be killed. That was terrible. I broke my heart! Betty grew up to have her own lambs, she was a Shropshire with a big fluffy face, Billy was a Kerry.

Della Pugh

The Farm had its own carpenter's shop and blacksmith's shop. Della Pugh, as a child living at The Farm, would spend time with the tradesmen.

I used to sit with Mr Fred Jones who was the local carpenter, undertaker and wheelwright in the carpenter's shop. The carpenter's shop was directly on the left as you go into the farmyard. There was a blacksmith's shop as well that dad had built, Tom Maun built it. There was everything in it, everything for a blacksmith. They used to make hoops to go round the wheels, Fred used to make the wheels. I pumped the bellows in the blacksmith's shop many times.

The age of machinery came to The Farm.

My dad had a lot of machinery put into The Farm, there was a big engine that ran things to save us doing it by hand, there was a big chaff cutter and a kibbler which kibbled (ground) wheat into flour and crushed oats. There was a big circular saw that came out through the wall and a big saw bench. The man who put it in fell backwards on it and cut his shoulder the day it was put in. Threshing days were great days, we hired the threshing machine from Mr Jones, The Hurst. Threshing would be a week at a time, old Joe Jones from Snailbeach always came with the threshing box. I would stand behind the little things with the shutters on that the bags were tied to, and the shutters would open to let the wheat through. I used to love that old engine....

Della Pugh

I was in the Land Army in the war. For my first job they put me on the threshing machine. I loved it. It was a three quarter threshing machine, not quite the full size. It was driven by a tractor. I was feeding the box. The box was set very level at the side of a corn barn. It's driven by belts from a tractor and there's a belt driving the baler. The corn is thrown up on to the box and the feeder, that's me, picks it up with a knife. You have a knife with a loop of string on your wrist and you twist the knife so the string breaks to scatter the sheaf on to the moving belt. You let it slide down your arm. Some people just cut the string and drop it and it goes 'zoomp', 'zoomp'. That is bad feeding and it doesn't thresh clean. If you trickle it down your arm, it slides down smoothly, very clean and threshes very fast. Threshing took place after the harvest through the winter, and you worked 'til dark. Another threshing machine job I had was with a steam engine. So when you were standing on the box you were in thick smoke. I used to consume two or three bottles of cough mixture each week. You wore goggles of course, otherwise you would have had no eyes! There was a driver for the engine and there was a second man. The second man left home at four-thirty in the morning to get the fire going to get steam up for when the driver arrived. I would get there a little later and there was always a can of tea keeping warm for me at the boiler end. They were very good to me. It could be raining, well I would cycle fifteen miles to stand in an open fronted implement shed to see if the rain cleared, and if it didn't you cycled fifteen miles back. You hadn't done any work so you didn't get any money, but you had cycled thirty miles. I got that I could look at a stack and assess to within a quarter of an hour how long it would take to thresh. Of course some of the stacks were full of thistles! You would spend an evening picking thistles out of your fingers. Sometimes at the bottom of a stack, when it got down to about two or three feet it was moving slowly up and down with rats underneath it! The men used to find pleasure in throwing the occasional rat's nest up on to the box and I, being the perfect lady that I am, used to find pleasure in throwing the little rats one by one back on to the men, which they didn't expect. They thought I'd have been frightened. If there were land girls on the farm, they were so rat conscious, if someone ran their finger up their leg they would scream ten thousand murders thinking it was a rat. But there was never really anything malicious, just good fun. Threshing days were the happiest days of my life.

Connie Read

Threshing machine (here working at Acton Scott)

The farmhouse was indeed the height of luxury compared to the basic squatters' cottages on the bleak hillside.

There was a big kitchen in the farmhouse, we were very lucky, we had hot and cold water. There was a huge double-sided range with a fire in the middle. There was a rack over the top and all the cooking pots which were all brass were kept on there. Mrs Morris used to clean them on a Friday. Mother would make rag rugs for the hearth and Mrs Morris would help her. We always lived in the kitchen on weekdays, but we always spent Sundays in the 'big kitchen' or the dining room, the grate in there was huge, you could put a hundredweight of coal on it at once! Above, it was open –

old Mr Sayce went up the chimney once to do something and mother had given him some rhubarb wine. He was drunk and black!

Each side of this great big open fire was a little oven and a hob.

We had the only telephone in the village for many years. The number was number 5 Minsterley. It was in the little parlour.

There was a well in the cellar at the farm and there was frogs in it. There were slate slabs on the floor.

Della pugh

Just as the novels of Thomas Hardy and Mary Webb would not be complete without a haystack on fire, so it was in Snailbeach, as Della Pugh explains.

There was the night the hay stack went on fire, a man came drunk, he broke all the windows in the front of the house with a stick. Annie Jones who lived in at the time knew who it was, he hit the back door with the stick and mother thought it was a gun! The marks were still on the back door when we left The Farm! Then he ran up in to the stack yard and set the stack on fire! The fire engines were horse drawn and had to come from Shrewsbury, they came and they stayed all night. All of the animals had to be moved out of the buildings because of the sparks. Sparks were flying and there was hay in the other buildings.

The police searched for him and found him at Shelfield, he was above the cow house in the hay with a bag over his head. They charged him with something, I don't know what!

Della Pugh

Sadly, Della Pugh's memorable childhood on The Farm in Snailbeach came to an abrupt and tragic end when her father was killed in an accident in Minsterley.

By the time I was 14, farming was in recession. We had to give up the farm when dad was killed. Loads of farmers were going bankrupt at the time. We had a farm sale and we moved down to one of the cottages and I had to go out to work, I went to clean in a little house in Birmingham.

Della Pugh

6: Sing to the Lord with cheerful voice

The old Cross Guns Inn at Crowsnest

Anyone unfamiliar with the district, might be forgiven for thinking there would have been precious little to do by way of entertainment in an isolated area like the Stiperstones in years gone by. Whilst 'leisure time' was limited, when an occasion for celebration or enjoyment did present itself it was entered into with gusto! Common factors seem to have been a local venue and local organisation. For many people trips to Shrewsbury for entertainment, or for any other reason, were rare events and a trip to the seaside notable indeed.

In the villages and hamlets of the Stiperstones, social life seemed to have centred largely around the village hall and the church or chapel. The area had a strong musical tradition (strengthened no doubt by the arrival of Welsh miners and engineers to work in the lead mines). There were a number of choirs, bands and musical groups – some well known locally for their skill and ability. When dances and concerts were held, the music was invariably provided by local players. This musical tradition still survives today, as does a strong sporting tradition.

There were a number of football teams in the area before the last war but the Snailbeach team was always the most renowned (and feared).

Pubs were also more numerous than they are today, though they were always largely the preserve of the men-folk. Memories still linger of the Miner's Arms at The Bog, The Cross Guns at Crowsnest and – going further back – The Crown at Pennerley. Games such as quoits and dominoes would help to while away an evening. The Miner's Arms at The Bog was, however, best known for the game of 'tippet' ...... and if you're not sure how that was played, then read on!

You met everybody at chapel

Sunday was a day for attending church or chapel and for quiet family pursuits.

You met everybody at chapel, you had a natter there. It was very much a social thing.

Sarah Ann Evans

If there was no chapel service on a Sunday evening, we'd go for a walk. It was lovely, mum, dad and all us children. We'd go down the Hopyard and out at the bottom on to the new road and back up the fields or we would go up the Crowsnest Dingle and up the Yethy Bank Rack up to the big chimney and back to the Crowsnest along the railway line.

Nellie Rowson

You could walk around on a Sunday afternoon and you would meet your neighbour and have a good talk with 'em. It was good – then you started having motorcars and instead of stopping and talking to your neighbour you just do your hand and keep on going.

Henry Owen

We had lovely dances at The Bog

Saturday night was the time when the young folk of the district (and the not so young) took to the dance floor.

We had lovely dances at The Bog. It was sixpence to go in. They used to play, Roll Along Covered Wagon, Roll Along, for a slow dance and if it was a quick-step they'd just play it faster!

When we were having dances in the club room at The Bog I can remember two ladies from The Bog turning up in the same dresses. They fought in the dance hall and the one went back and changed! And they were friends!

We had skirts and blouses for the dances, mum made some, we made some at school. We used to go to Woolworths or Bishops Castle for clothes. If we had one new outfit it had to last for a long while. It didn't matter you went in the same thing.

We used to bike miles to dances as well, from The Bog to Wentnor was nothing, we would to the Gravels across Shelve Hill, go to the More Arms and then to the Gravels dance and walk back home after. It was fun. At the local dances they had waltzing competitions and spot dances which made it interesting. I remember being at a dance at The Bog school and we were only school children twelve or thirteen and I ended up fighting with a girl over a boy, Harvey Mountford. This girl took a fancy to him and tried to take him off me and I wasn't having any of that! We had a little argy-bargy at the dance 'cos she wouldn't leave him alone! We had only ever passed little notes to each other at school. We were very naive in those days.

Millie Gough

The Bog clubroom

Music was provided by local people who had the ability and the confidence to perform in public.

There was the local Bog dance. Clifford Lewis' dad used to play the drums. Dave Faulkner used to play the piano, and when he couldn't come, Joe Evans from Shelve used to play. There was only the drums and the piano and that was it. It was surprising how many people used to get there. People'd walk for miles from Snailbeach and the Gravels. It was a big night and the pub would be packed out.

Roly Johnson

I remember Mr Evans from Shelve playing Horsey,Horsey don't you stop, just let your feet go clippety clop.......... we used to do the Palais Glide to that and there'd be Coming Round the Mountain...... and The Wheel of the Wagon is Broken and it aint going to turn no more.......... and Little Angeline.......

Susie Hartshorn

There was dances at The Bog every fortnight which was a highlight of our fortnight throughout my teens and twenties. The band was a piano, a piano accordion and a drum.

The dance was in the club room. It was only a tin shack but quite a reasonable place. They had a games room there, for a few years we used to go in the early forties. It was only open one or two nights a week. There were two billiard tables and table tennis.

Henry Jones

Youngsters wanting to attend the dances had to rely on local bus services and 'shanks's pony' for transport.

They'd have a dance at Snailbeach one weekend then the next Saturday night they'd have it at The Bog and sometimes they'd have one at the Gravels. We'd come up on Swain's bus from Minsterley and walk home to Horsebridge. The bus would get to Minsterley at ten o'clock at the Bath Arms on a Saturday night and he'd have a full load. You'd have to stand and everyone was nursing one another. It was only a little twenty seater bus and it would be choc-a-bloc. Doreen Swain would have an awful job to get round to take the fares off 'em.

Les Hordley

We didn't have entertainment very often. There was usually a concert first which the locals would entertain with. It was all amateur and some of it was not very good, I can tell you! And then there'd be a dance after. My father-in-law played for the dances. He played the piano and he always finished at twelve o'clock because he had to walk back to Shelve. The lads would come down from the hills in their hob nail boots and dance in them, they'd dance in anything, those days, and it was dancing then, not like it is today. We used to enjoy that.

Sarah Ann Evans

For teenage girls, the dances were a particular treat but keeping to the rules laid down by their parents was still of considerable importance.

I learnt to dance in the school yard at the Stiperstones. After that there were some dancing classes in the room behind the Cross Guns pub at the Crowsnest. They used to have dances in there, it was grand. Mind you, our dad was strict, he'd be at the gate to see us coming out 'cos we only lived *the other side of the road. He'd be there to see if anybody ever took me home. I'd be fourteen or fifteen then. It was wonderful to go to those dances. We would wind the gramophone up, Peggy o'Neil was a girl that could steal, they were wonderful tunes. I could do 'the Lancers', 'the Bluebird' all those dances that we did in those days. I must have been a frivolous little bit of stuff!*

No – I never was frivolous, I hadn't got the face to go with it! I was lucky to get a partner sometimes, but never mind, when I did I enjoyed it!

Mollie Rowson

We were about fourteen or fifteen and we used to go to the dances at The Bog – we could go up on the bus at seven o'clock but it was a bit early for the dance so we went in The Bog pub, we didn't go drinking! Somebody went and told Nurse Hand and she came and told my mum about me, I could never go again and I never forgave her.

Mary Challinor

For teenage boys of any generation, the subject of 'girls' could prove to be something of a mystery – and a challenge.

I was only young then reading the Womans Weekly to find out about females what I could – the letters they used to write used to fascinate me! I used to think, what the hell is that? I thought well they're certainly different to us, girls are. I found out by the time I was about fourteen!

We would walk down to Minsterley to a dance, get a pint on the slate down there, create mayhem and stagger back.

Walton Humphrey

Nobody travelled very far in them days, not even to go courting, just as far as you could bike.

Jack Pugh

We did have some funny cars

Transport came in many different guises.

There wasn't much traffic on the road then. If you sat out-side Minsterley school all day when I went there I expect only about ten vehicles would go past, not many more. You'd see delivery vans and Sentinel steam wagons taking meal to the farms and the big heavy traffic would be the iron wheeled stone wagons going up to the Waterwheel or

Snailbeach. The road to Snailbeach would be a dust trap. A lot of folks would come and meet the train at Minsterley Station with horses and traps. There would be a carrier cart that would come down to take folks to Snailbeach or Hope.

Jack Pugh

As cars became more readily available in the 1920s and 30s, they were for some the preferred mode of transport. But the journeys were not without incident.

We had this old three wheeler car and we used to go to dances at The Bog and at the Gravels and perhaps we'd be driving to The Bog and all of a sudden the lights would turn round and be facing you. They were loose and I'd have to get out and twiddle them.

We bought another old car, a 1934 Austin, and coming up Longfield Terrace it started to pour with rain and it was raining in. So Betty put the umbrella up in the car so who should we meet but Thelma and Mervyn Bonner on their motorbike – we never lived it down!

I used to go to work from the White Banks in this Austin 10 every morning – one morning we got down to the little bridge on the main road at Plox Green. I said to George Edwards, who was with me, "There's a wheel going down there!". Just now the car dropped – we'd lost our front wheel, it was going down the road in front of us!

Les Hordley

I was about sixteen or seventeen with an old car and was off down to the Tankerville shop one morning. I stopped to give owd Mr Smout a lift. He did'na want to get in, he'd never bin in a car. He'd only ever bin to Minsterley twice and Shrewsbury once in his life and he was in his seventies! He would'na get in the front so he got in the back and I tore off down to Tankerville. When we got there I turned round and there was no sign of Mr Smout he was laid on the floor behind the seat – terrified!

Barry Jones

I remember the first vehicle we ever had. It was a Commer van with sacking in the windows. The trouble was you usu-ally had to get the horse to tow it to get it to start.

John Bennett

Locally run buses, no matter how 'rough and ready', provided a vital service for the people of the Stiperstones.

George Williams had a haulage business up the Ventor. He had a lorry that would lug barytes down to Minsterley during the week but on a Saturday he would fasten a container with windows in it on the flat bottomed lorry. He would then take people to shop in Shrewsbury.
Graham France

I remember the first bus, and that was started off by Mr Edwin Hotchkiss from the Cold Hill, him and his son had an old lorry and they put a body on it and two seats across, so the people sat facing one another. That was the first Bog bus and the exhaust pipe used to blow in the dirt. I remember us going with Snailbeach Choral Union, and my father-in-law was conductor and there were sixty voices. We were going to compete in Shrewsbury, there'd been a carnival and there was an Eisteddfodd after it in the Market Hall. Anyway, we went in this bus with this exhaust pipe blowing on us, and when we got out we were black. We had to go and get a wash. We went to what was then the County Cafe to get some of it off before performing.
Sarah Ann Evans

Edwin Davies from Snailbeach had a carriers cart that would take people up and down to Minsterley station.
Mary Challinor

Edwin Davies and his carrier cart in Snailbeach

Grandad was a carrier. I was three or four and would go with him to meet the train with a horse and trap and the owd horse would stop outside the Bath Arms and wouldn't move waiting for him to come out. My grandfather told me as how he would take the bosses from the mine round other sites and quarries and the horse would bring them back in the trap at night. They'd all be paralytic and her'd come back on her own. One night my grandmother couldn't manage to get him out of the trap and she threatened to saw the shafts off. Anyway she didna, she took the harness off the horse and pulled it out tipping the trap up and him out over the back!
Tom Pinches

We had the silent pictures

For the more adventurous, a return trip on the Minsterley branch railway ensured a good night out in the county town of Shrewsbury, including perhaps a moving picture.

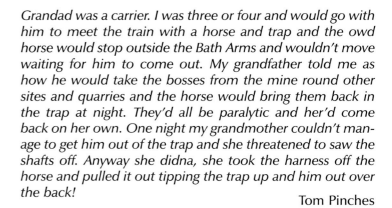
Minsterley Railway Station

It was 7d return to Shrewsbury on the train and as I was getting a bit older you went into town on a Saturday night and went for a drink in the Market Vaults, you'd come out of there and go into the County Theatre, right up in the flea rack or whatever they called it! 4d that was. Then you went back out on the train – you could always catch the train, folks knew the drivers and they used to tell 'em to hang on and they would, to quarter to twelve some nights. There was always some porters on duty even coming home at that time of night – I can hear 'em now and see the little owd lantern he was carrying.

The first moving picture I ever saw was Noel Coward's Cavalcade. I know one picture everyone went to see was Journey's End.

Jack Pugh

At one time, the 'movies' were also available more locally.

We had the silent pictures in Minsterley parish hall in the 1930s – The Keystone Cops – somebody would boom away on the piano. It was on a couple of nights a week. We'd sneak in there sometimes in the moonlight, open the top door and you'd see all the folks sitting there – staring.

Jack Pugh

Once a year we'd go to the sea

A trip to the seaside was a relatively rare event and eagerly anticipated. Having money in your pocket to spend meant putting in some hard work beforehand.

Once a year we'd go to the sea and we would have to pick whinberries and blackberries to get spending money. If you told kids these days that they had to go and pick blackberries or shoot rabbits to go out for a day – well!

I picked blackberries and sold them to Lewis' of Gorsty Bank at 3d a pound. We made enough money to hire a car to go to Aberystwyth for the day. I was driving then, well I don't know if they relished the thought of me driving, but they were alright.

Aunty Harriet said she felt ill when we got to Aberystwyth, so we went and got her some brandy in a little bottle. There was a fly in the bottle, anyway she got underneath the blanket in the back of the car and drunk the brandy. Well, the fly went anyway! I don't think they'd come across anything quite like me, because I got in the sea at Aberystwyth and swam. They must have thought, whatever has our Graham got hold of!

Mavis France

I was probably fifteen the first time I ever went to the seaside.

Henry Jones

"Once a year we'd go to the sea", including Mrs Jack Hughes and Jack, Wilfred Dean and Flossie.

I fell in love with the Stiperstones. Here I would wish to dwell.

Whilst Stiperstones people might look to the coast for a change of scene, for others the Stiperstones was itself a holiday destination. Jeanette and Dorothea Merry were sisters from the south of England, but regular visitors to the Stiperstones and well known to many of the residents, particularly at the southern end of the range. In 1948 they rented a tiny stone cottage known as The Rock Cottage, not far from Black Rhadley hill. There they spent many happy holidays. On retirement, the sisters came to live at The Square, Minsterley.

There was not a house in sight nor sign of habitation, only God's earth created as at the beginning: timeless, peaceful, soul-satisfying. I fell in love with the Stiperstones. Here I would wish to dwell.

From "The Rock" by Jeanette Merry

In their younger days, the Miss Merrys – as they were almost universally known – had been fond of camping.

The Miss Merrys, they used to come and camp at Rigmoreoak – till Topsy sat on their tent. We had a horse with a deformed foot. Of course, we thought the world of this horse, she used to turn her one back leg in, she was born like it. She very rarely lied down but she used to sit down quite a lot, and one night she sat on the Miss Merrys' tent – when they were in it! They came down to dad and said, "Mr Hotchkiss, could you please come and move your horse, she's sitting on our tent".

Sybil Cook

There we slept on camp beds in the heather, and the brilliant stars seemed to drop out of a dark purple velvet sky on to us. Each night we saw shooting stars. Sheep were our only companions and the call of the grouse,
"Go back, go back, go back"
our waking alarm....... In the morning we found we had left most of the records lying on the ground and as sheep were wandering close to us, one was licking a record, I got up to rescue them. I found two were broken, the sheep having walked over them, one of which was, believe it or not, 'All we like sheep have gone astray'!

From "The Rock" by Jeanette Merry

For Walton Humphrey, life at the Stiperstones Inn meant making sacrifices to maximise the number of paying guests accommodated.

Mother used to rely on the visitors, we used to have the place full. We would be sleeping in the garden shed so she could make money in the summer months. They used to advertise in the Liverpool Echo, bed and breakfast, lunch and evening meal. There was a huge dining room table with a white cloth on it of course, and mother had a little dustpan and brush for the table, you couldn't take those huge tablecloths off everytime you got crumbs on them, so I had that little job to brush the crumbs off after the toast had been served in the toast racks, with all the crusts cut off of course.

The Stiperstones Inn

Weddings – a new coat and a little bit of a party at home

The wedding day was not an extravagant occasion.

There was no weddings at the local chapels, my sister was married at Bishops Castle. I was married at Marton Chapel. It was the done thing in those days to go to Marton. There wasn't much finery about, I had nothing special, a new coat, and then we'd have a little bit of a party at home. We hadn't the money to go to Shrewsbury to buy an outfit or anything, you just had your best dress that you'd got. I had one bridesmaid, she just had her own best clothes on and that was it. We never had a holiday after. I was only nineteen when I got married.

Sarah Ann Evans

Weddings would be very much a family do, they'd be doing their own food, perhaps using the local village hall but people tended to make their own wedding parties in their own homes with just close family. There wasn't the money about for anything else.

Derek Rowson

I first met Eva on a bus going to Shrewsbury. We got married in 1943 at Bishops Castle Registry Office. I came home on leave on the Tuesday and went back on the Saturday morning. Some neighbours had clubbed together and I think they boiled a ham and did a bit of a get-together at home. That was on the Friday and I went back on the Saturday morning to West Kirby for embarcation to the Far East.

Bernard Millington

Bernard and Eva Millington on their wedding day, 2nd April 1943

It was a red letter day to go to Minsterley Show

In the year 2000, Minsterley show celebrated its 125th anniversary. The show has a proud record of having survived two World Wars, flood, drought and epidemic. It is remembered fondly as one of the highlights of the year.

It was a red letter day to go to Minsterley Show. It was marvellous to go to the Show. You only went if you was lucky enough to have the money. If you was lucky enough to pick whinberries on the hill and have the money, you could go to the show.
Mollie Rowson

Minsterley sports and show were big days of the year. The show was on the third Thursday in August and the sports day was August Bank Holiday Monday, always. We used to have our new finery for them. The chapels used to have their new clothes for the anniversaries, we would have them for the show. It was great. Mother used to make our hats and dresses, there were swing boats, hobbie horses, the usual things. The horse race went from the Parish Hall and around the fields. There were bookies. Our white horse Nobby, they put him in the show, but mother had to keep well out of the way, he'd run to her if he saw her because she had hand reared him. Freda, Sweet Crystal and White Sock were all ponies that ran in the races. My brothers used to ride the ponies in the races.
Della Pugh

People remained in a sessile state over tea for a very long time while the chief race of the afternoon was begun by the ringing of the dinner-bell. The race took so long, the riders having to go round the course so many times, that people went on complacently with their tea, only looking out occasionally to see how things progressed, watching the riders go by – one with bright red braces, one in a blue cotton coat, two middle aged men in their best bowlers, and one, obviously too well mounted for the rest, in correct riding-dress. They came around each time in the same order – the correct one, red braces, blue coat and the bowlers last. Evidently the foremost one knew he could easily win, and the others had decided that 'it was to be'. In the machine like regularity of their advent, their unaltered positions, and leisured pace, they were like hobby-horses.
From Gone to Earth by Mary Webb

I always remember the cart-horse race

Snailbeach also had its own annual show – well known for its sports and horse racing.

Mrs O'Halloran used to open the Sports Day, 'Babs' O'Halloran. She came from Ireland and she always wore white and she bought the Smelthouse off Tom Oldfield.
I always remember the cart-horse race – Gilbert Hotchkiss had a white horse of Sandells' and Stanley Evans from Shelfield, was on one of his own. Gilbert beat Stanley; those great big horses, they were about 20 hands, they were huge! There was no saddles on 'em, just bare back. There was a ditch in the field, I can see these horses going through the ditch! Tommy Griffiths would bring his lads up from Minsterley and there'd be Wynnes and the Phillips' from Hogstow and they'd all race around the field. There'd be prize money but no betting.
Doug Boulter

The adults came into their own, all dressing up for the carnival with the children. There would be three legged races, egg and spoon races. It always took several men to put the Union Jack up. There would be tents and marquees all on the football field below the church.
Derek Rowson

"Miss Peace" at Snailbeach Carnival circa 1946

Earlier in the year and a little further afield was the May Fair at Bishops Castle. The fair traditionally took place on the first Friday in May and had its origins as a hiring fair for local farm workers and live-in servants.

We used to go to Bishops Castle May Fair and very often had to walk from The Bog to the Castle and back of course. There was roundabouts and different side shows and things like that. It was good.

Sarah Ann Evans

The fair at Bishop's Castle was the highlight of the year. It was just a May Fair with all the rides and side shows. To get a boy friend and go there was most romantic. You'd get the boys shooting for something and win you a nice fluffy toy. We had some lovely times there. We've been wet a few times when it poured with rain and you've been paddling around in rain and mud and still enjoying it. It was where the cattle market is now. They used to do a parade through the street with the organs, the music from the organs was beautiful. We would be saving up for the May Fair for months before, and if you hadn't got a boyfriend it was a little bit of a problem, because that made the fun. If you could go, three or four girls and three or four lads, you could have a real good laugh shying at the coconuts, going in the swing boats to see who could go the highest and who'd be the sickest after.

Millie Gough

There was a colt fair in Bishops Castle in October each year, dad would always take us to that, we'd have to have a day off school for that.

Jim Booth

GOLDEN GALLOPING HORSE

— MAY FAIR

Play up the Stars

Football on the Stiperstones has a long history. In the days when the mines were operating, many of the mining villages had their own teams – notable amongst them were Hopesgate, The Bog and Snailbeach. The present Snailbeach club dates back to the 1940s and in its day was one of the leading teams in local amateur football. Today it still survives, and owns its own ground on the edge of the village.

We started in 1943 with twelve months' friendlies before we went in a league. I was at the very first meeting, Jack Poole was the chairman, Tom Jones was the secretary, Eric Jones was the treasurer – I was on the committee. A year later Joe Rowson took over as chairman for the next twelve months, then my brother in law asked me to be chairman and I did it for the next forty years! We took the name from the old team The Snailbeach White Stars.

We played on the field just below the church, changing in the village hall where we had a tin bath and cold water to wash in.

We had a job to move with the mud – it'd be over your ankles and we had a heavy leather ball that'd knock your brains out.

Snailbeach White Stars Football Club 1910-1911

A lot of the women turned out to raise money by running dances once a fortnight at Snailbeach and organising a Christmas draw. They would also make the teas and wash the kit.

The committee of 16 met every Monday at Snailbeach and there were some good arguments over who was going to play.

Harry Trow

It was 1943 when my brother John and I were asked to come and play for Snailbeach. There was Joe and Clayton Rowson, Trafford Williams, George Swain and Fred Jones, Tom Purslow and 'Happy' Adams. We won everything there was to win, we were 'in charge' in the South Shropshire League.

Harold Hartshorn

The White Stars Football Club – 1946

Committee (at back) Tom Jones (secretary), Jack Poole (president), Matthew Jones (trainer), Harry Trow (chairman), Alfred Adams (member), Eric Davies (treasurer), Clayton Rowson (player and substitute on this day).

Team, back row: Joe Rowson, Harold Hartshorn, Fred Jones, George Griffiths, Bert Jones.

Front row: Ivor Lewis, Harold Hill (goalie), John Hartshorn, Don Rowson, Trafford Williams, Mick Curley.

I started playing for Snailbeach in 1948 or '49 with Jock Donaldson, Graham France, Pop Lewis, Harold Hartshorn, Bob Lloyd and John Hartshorn. They'd have three or four coach loads of spectators for a cup match. They'd be all around the pitch, three or four deep, especially for the Ludlow and Bishops Castle Cups.

They played just down below St Luke's church on the field on the left hand side – it was very wet. You had high topped boots in those days and you'd be in mud three inches deep. As you came off the pitch there was a little brook went down the middle of the field so you would stand in that to get the worst of the mud off your boots. Then we would go up to the village hall for a cup of tea, a sandwich and a cake which the women always put on for us. There was no showers in those days you had a wash when you got home.

They entered a lot of cups in those days Ludlow, Knighton, Clee Hill, Bishops Castle and then there was the league cup. Sometimes you'd finish up playing five games in a week towards the end of the season if you had a good run in the cups. We played two matches in one day, the Bishops Castle Cup and the Knighton Cup and we won them both. We had Billy Hailstone's coach years ago to go to the away matches. It was always full.

I played at Hopesgate for a while and we had a bloke who worked on the coal lorry – he was always playing in goal and if it started to rain, the coal dust used to run down his face, he never feared anything, he'd come out of goal and go at their feet, his face all black! I think he used to frighten them more than anything.

The balls in them days were leather with a leather lace and if you headed the ball and got it on the lace you knew about it! When it rained, the ball would carry the water and it would be that heavy. We went to Craven Arms to play in a cup match and it snowed and the ball was picking up all the snow.

The football boots were leather and had got hard toe caps. We had to make our own studs, we'd buy leather studs with nails in and you'd be knocking them in on a Saturday morning.

Very rare you had a booking or a sending off. Lads would be a bit rough in the game but they'd all come off shaking *hands. They never beared no malice. The ref would speak to you like but that would be the end of it.*

Les Hordley

If Snailbeach played Pontesbury or Hanwood it was a big match it was very rare they could beat Pontesbury. But I remember once they had the game in the evening after the sports day they had to play Pontesbury in the League and Snailbeach won! It was a fantastic day and there was a good crowd because people stayed over from the sports day.

Doug Boulter

The half-time whistle meant some welcome refreshment.

Lydie used to make the coffee and she'd take it down in a big tin thing and give the men the coffee at half time. They were doing evaporated milk at the Creamery and she'd make it with that. If you worked there you could buy dented tins at 3d a tin, if I remember right. We used to call it 'shake well' cos on the top of the little tins it had 'shake well'

Elsie Rowson

The Snailbeach team and supporters even had their own song to help while away coach journeys to and from away games and, of course, to help celebrate famous victories.

Play up the Stars, the jolly old Stars,
The forwards are smart on the ball,
The half backs and full backs want beating, want beating,
But the goalie they can't beat at all!
Good old Snailbeach by the sea!
Good old Snailbeach by the sea!
For they'll rue the day they played away,
At Snailbeach by the sea!

As sung by Les and Betty Hordley

And what goals they hadn't scored on the Saturday.............

Tom Jones from the Lordshill was secretary of the football team and mother always used to get some bread for him from the baker and he'd fetch it on a Sunday morning. Well that was cup of tea time wasn't it? There'd be dad, Harold and Johnny and Tom, the house would be full and what goals they hadn't scored on the Saturday they'd score on the Sunday!

Susie Hartshorn

A penny a pint!

For Walton Humphrey, growing up at the Stiperstones Inn meant early responsibility on young shoulders.

I was head barman at about twelve years of age. All the Rowsons used to come in and haunt us. Mother'd go down to St Luke's Church and say, "I'm off to church now, see you get these men out." Well there was some chance of that wasn't there?

"Let's have a Woodbine", they'd say, "Go on swallow the smoke". And I did and the room started to spin and I would go green and they'd say, "Have half a pint, go on it wunna hurt ya – get it down ya!" Mother'd come back from church having walked down there and back and say, "What are these men still doing here?"

"Oh it's all right Esther, don't worry about it – he's been a good lad", and they'd soothe her down. She'd be baking her bread and they'd be eating it hot out of the oven and sometimes she'd leave a great big joint of beef in the oven and the older Rowsons would get it out and take slices off it. They would get furiously drunk.

The beer had to be fetched from the cellar every time, my poor little old legs. I don't know if I was in full control at twelve but one night they were drinking after time, we'd close at ten, I was coming up the cellar steps with a tray full of glasses of beer and old George Evans grabbed hold of me, "Copper coming!". So of course I went back down the stairs.

Bitter was in bottles, Indian Pale Ale made by Worthingtons. Southams used to brew a mild beer, it was straight from the wood. We'd have nine gallon kegs all stretched out in the cellar. I learnt a lot – I could tap a barrel, you'd take the bung out and hammer the tap in. A pint of Southams beer was 6d and ten Woodbines 4d. Spirits were off the old fashioned optics with the pewters. You'd have a pewter to measure gin, whisky or brandy. We had a wooden till with four little sections. Mother had to watch it very closely because father would go in there, short of money, and take a pound out for petrol. The book keeping methods weren't so hot.

I saw Don and Norman Rowson have a row there once which was unusual because they were very very close as brothers. By God, they decided to have a fight this one day and there was me collecting all the glasses off the tables because they were hammering hell out of each other.

Walton Humphrey

At the Stiperstones Inn they used to fetch the beer up from the cellar. 'Cocky' Roberts and one or two others used to go rather late, being farmers, and then they liked to stop late. So Winnie would leave the cellar door open and they would go down and help themselves and leave the money.

Graham France

The isolated remains of the old Crown Inn still stand today on the hillside above Pennerley. The pub closed in the very early years of the 20th century, but its reputation lives on.

There was a pub at Pennerley – the Crown – it was going when all the miners lived up there. It was said they could hear for a mile the miners singing in the Crown on a Saturday night. Mrs Chidley kept the Crown and she used to sweep the beer that had been spilt on the floor out through the door with a broom after they'd gone at eleven or twelve o'clock at night and they couldn't afford to spill it like that today! They say it was a penny a pint then.

Henry Jones

The Crown at Pennerley was kept by Chidleys and men used to come from the Bridges for bare knuckle fights.

Les Hotchkiss

For young men (even those with long trousers), paternal discipline in matters of drink was a force to be reckoned with.

I always remember having my first long trousers, I was about fifteen. If you had long trousers you could get in the pub in Minsterley. It was after a Sunday school anniversary and we all went down to Minsterley to the Bridge [pub]. There used to be a quoit board in the Bridge and above it was a lot of bottles. We must have had a couple of halves and got a bit foolish playing with the quoits, instead of them going on the board we was throwing them at the bottles and knocking them off the shelf. We got barred! I came home that night and my father said, "Are you all right?" I told him, "I've sold this suit for two and six!"

Now drink was forbidden in our home and he realised that I had been drinking so I was grounded yet again.

Graham France

The night life was at The Miners' Arms

Up at The Bog the two centres for social life were the 'Miners' Welfare' or clubhouse and the Miners' Arms pub. The Miners' Arms survived the closure of many other small public houses and was still in use as recently as the early 1960s.

The Miners' Arms was a wonderful meeting place. If you lived on the estate you would have to go to pay your rent there, an agent would come to collect the rent and three parts of the tenants would get drunk that day.

We played dominoes and quoits, there wasn't much else for anyone to go to, it was just for men. There was just beer to drink, and they could drink too.

We used to play tippet for hours. Some got very clever at it, you'd stare at their faces trying to put them off.

Henry Owen

The Miners Arms

The Miners' Arms was a rare place in the old days, we had a tippet team there. There used to be a tippet supper. A tippet was a button. There'd be four or five men on each side and one would have the button and they'd put their hands on the table and the opposite team had got to guess who'd got the button. There was some very good tippet players, they'd study the expressions on people's faces.

Les Hotchkiss

The only qualification I've got is that I was a good tippet player.
Clifford Lewis

Every other weekend they used to reckon the ditches down from The Bog pub would be running with blood! I think that was a slight exaggeration. The Gravels hut – that was another good place for a fight.
Jim Booth

The local constabulary adopted something of a 'hands off' approach to hostelries on the higher reaches of the Stiperstones. There was still respect, however, for the authority they represented.

The police didn't have a lot of problems in this area, there was quite a lot of drunkeness but you could get fined for not having a dog licence or riding a bike with no lights. I got pinched by the 'special' Jim Price and P.C. Arkinstall for having no lights on my bike and I got fined ten bob.

The policeman from Bishops Castle called at the Miners' Arms one night, late, and as he walked through the door they popped their pints in the oven. We got warned not to stay so late. It was a good fighting place at The Bog, the police kept clear but then people respected the policeman and we was frittened to death of him.
Clifford Lewis

Any woman that went to the pub was a slut!

As elsewhere, long tradition dictated that the pubs and clubs of the area were largely the preserve of the men-folk. Women who ventured in took a serious risk with their reputation.

There was a fish and chip shop at Crowsnest kept by Mrs Preece. Around the back of the Cross Guns pub was a club house with a billiard table. There was another club house at the Tankerville and one at The Bog. The clubs used to play one another in billiard tournaments.

They didn't serve alcohol in these club houses. I don't even remember any soft drinks. My father would take me on a Saturday night to the club at the Tankerville. He was secretary or treasurer. They also played dominoes and games like that. It was men only – no ladies. They would be at

home doing the housework. Any woman that went to the pub was a slut! But then the war changed everything.
Graham France

The Cross Guns Pub

There was dances at the men's club at The Bog, women were allowed to the dances, but they were not allowed in the club room when they was playing billiards and that.
Henry Owen

My dad wasn't a pub man. There was a pub at The Bog, the Miners' Arms. Mrs Sandells was the landlady, she would be serving. Oh no, women didn't go to the pub, no you were a real slut if you went to the pub! Her character went down if ever a women was seen in the pub, even with her husband. Some women would occasionally go but they would be thought very little of. The women stopped at home doing their mending or whatever they had to do.
Sarah Ann Evans

Women didn't go to the pubs, not before the Second World War. They wouldn't be very highly thought of.
Jack Pugh

There was whist drives in the hut

The plans for a village hall at Snailbeach were drawn up in September 1933 at a cost of ten shillings. Meetings and money raising efforts took place in a club room behind the Cross Guns public house in Crowsnest. Fund raising events included dances, whist drives and even a 'smoking concert' that raised six shillings and tuppence in November 1933.

It was always said that a Mr Gray who owned and worked the area called Gray's Works, in the mining times, now the children's play area, gave the land to the village on which to build the hut. From the records it appeared the committee were paying Mr Gray rent of five shillings per year in 1939. However, in June 1946 the village hall is recorded as holding the deeds to the land.

In December 1936 the sum of two pounds ten shillings and five pence was paid to A Bertram Edwards for timber for a wash-house that was put at the end of the hut. The Snailbeach football teams used it for their baths after they had finished their matches, the first one was lucky, he had clean water in the tin bath!

Snailbeach Village Hall, Coronation Day 1936

The hut was finished in 1937 and boasted a coal stove and oil lamps, the lavatory was outside. The hall was then used on occasions by the Liberal Party, the Methodist and Baptist congregations. The Home Guard used the premises during the war years and there is a record of the blackout paper roll costing two shillings. Whist drives and dances were really popular during the war years and continued afterwards to be well attended village events. Whist prizes included geese, ducks, rabbits, chickens and cigarettes.

Margaret Price

Even today, whist drives survive as a form of entertainment and an excuse for a social gathering. In years gone by, nearly every village would have its own whist drive.

There was whist drives in the hut at Snailbeach. Poultry whist drives all around Christmas and people would go to win their Christmas dinner. They were at Snailbeach, The Bog, The Waterwheel, Minsterley, the Gravels, the Grit, Priestweston and Churchstoke. They went from early December to the big one on December the 24th. Women played at the whist drives, in fact everybody would go.

Doug Boulter

Perhaps not surprisingly, they could also provide an excuse for mischief for local lads.

There was a 'jenny' for the electricity in a little tin shed at the hut, and at the whist drives it would go bump and the 'jenny' would stop, and poor old Gilbert Hotchkiss would say, "Those flinking lads, they've gone and switched the engine off again!" Then they'd be playing whist and the hut had one of these round stoves with the chimney up through the roof and Jim Simcox would let us get up on his shoulders and we'd put a clod on the chimney. "Oh them flinking lads have done it again!", said Gilbert. There was a flue to this fire and we used to piddle down the flue and Gilbert would shout, "Them flinking lads have piddled on the fire!"

Doug Boulter

Brass instruments....all polished and shiny

The people of the Stiperstones were rightly proud of having a strong musical tradition. Then, as now, brass bands were an important form of activity for some – and entertainment for others.

I was at school when I first started playing instruments. My father and three of my brothers were in the Brass Band. We would bike down to Snailbeach to practise in the school room over on the works. The conductor was Bert Rowson from the old Snailbeach Post Office. There was three brothers, Bert used to play and conduct and Jack used to play the trombone. There was a lot of young lads in the band in those days. 'Happy' Adams played in it, but it all packed up around 1936.

Somebody asked my father to get the band going again, so he did, and we would practise in the front room at The Green. 'Wigan' Will was a very good euphonium player from Hemford and he came over to conduct us.

At the same time my brother George was working as a chauffeur for Max Wenner at Batchcott Hall and he got a band going over there. Heber Rowson and I would bike over after school on a Friday to practise with them. They'd got a uniform and all. I went for private music tuition in Annscroft.

We always got regular jobs on a Good Friday and a Whit Monday at the parades from the Baptist and Methodist chapels. The band would play in different places, Crowsnest, Lordshill and the top of the bank, where the kids would have a scramble for sweets and nuts. There would be a tea party afterwards. I can remember playing in a field at Westbury and at Middletown and in a British Legion parade at Hope. My father, George, Wallace, Heber, 'Happy' Adams, Fred Jones and Wilson Morgan would all be playing. If we

The first Snailbeach Band – early 1900's

were playing anywhere away, the girls at home would have to polish the brass instruments and we'd go down the road on our bikes with our instruments on our backs all polished and shiny.

I eventually ended up with the big drum but it finished up in the coal house, and I think I burnt it in the end. The Snailbeach and District Band finished in 1936, the war finished it. Before the war there were quite a few bands about, there was one at Longden and one at Wattlesborough. We'd go and help the other bands out if they'd got an engagement and they wanted extra players. Records show that there was a band in the area as early as 1911.

There was a band playing in the film Gone to Earth in 1949, but I think they actually came from Condover.

Bill Evans

Small groups of players would also play at dances and were much in demand.

I used to play in the band for dances at The Bog with Jack Evans, Bill Evans, Fred Jones and Harold Evans. I played the cornet, I was about twelve or fourteen. Mr Evans used to play the piano, he used to play Roll Along Covered Wagon *which was THE song then. So, for every dance you had Roll Along Covered Wagon. If it was a slow foxtrot, it would be played slow, and if it was a quick step, you would speed it up! We would play from Hemford down to Hope church at Easter. We practised at the Stiperstones every Sunday morning and other nights in the week.*

Graham France

One dance band was called "The Rhythm Boys", and in that was Frank Swain on saxaphone, Fred Jones on trumpet, Bert Evans from Pontesbury on the accordion and Johnny Swain was the drummer, later on Wilson Morgan was the pianist.

Bill Evans

It was a singing district

Choirs of all kinds also played an important role in the social fabric of the area. They would travel over a wide area for the opportunity to perform.

My husband had three choirs at one time: a Juvenile Choir from the Stiperstones school that used to go into competitions, and he had the Lordshill Choir, and the Snailbeach Choral Union. It was a singing district.

We used to come down to the old school room on the Works to practise in the choir, that was our recreation. We practised twice a week Sunday and Wednesday, we all used to meet up and have a bit of fun going home.
Sarah Ann Evans

I was in Snailbeach male voice choir. We sang at chapels. We were pretty strong, we didn't enter competitions it was just for concerts and chapels.
Wallace Evans

There was a choir at Pennerley and I sung alto in that choir when I was eight.

Once I had to sing at the Sylvester Horne Institute in Church Stretton in front of Kenneth Horne's mother, who sat on the stage. I had to sing with Teddy Cowell who was an outstanding singer. Joe Evans had trained him and we sang The Old Rugged Cross.
Clifford Lewis

In later years Clifford's singing, and that of his friends, was a great hit in the local pubs and elsewhere.

There were concert parties, with singing and a play. We'd travel round giving these concerts, even to the Granary at Coates Farm. We were known as 'The Bog Mountaineers', me and Teddy Perkin sung Cut Down The Old Pine Tree *and George Bennett would sing* Two Little Girls In Blue. *If we sang in the pub they'd be standing on the tables.*
Clifford Lewis

Gone to Earth

The summer of 1949 saw memorable events taking place on the Stiperstones. Mary Webb (1881-1927), who lived in Shropshire, had written *Gone to Earth*, a novel which was being made into a film. Much of the filming took place in Much Wenlock, Longnor Hall, Pontesford Hill and the area around Lordshill Baptist Chapel above Snailbeach.

Well known Hollywood film-makers Michael Powell and Emeric Pressburger were behind the venture and they brought with them filmstars David Farrar, Cyril Cusack and Jennifer Jones. Many local people were recruited as 'extras' and – dressed in period costumes from the 1890s – had a wonderful time taking part in what must have seemed a glorious, unexpected adventure.

The cast of "Gone to Earth"
From top left: Alice Rowson, Wilfred Purslow, Lily Jones, Doris Purslow, Eunice Davies, Ruth Davies, Gwen Adams, Lily Hotchkiss, Chrissie Rowson, Eva Bailey, Sarah-Ann Evans, Joe Evans, Elsie Williams, Dorothy Rowson, Silvia Jones, Thelma Harrison, Jose Evans, W. Prose, Betty Davies, Annie Parry, Millie Evans, Clifford Lewis, Wilfred Dean, Margret Price, Rose Edwards, Francis Edwards, Mavis France, Doreen Rowson, Charlie Hayward, Lily Crowther, Doug Jones, L. Hayward, Beatty Jones and the filmcrew.

It was a big thing for the area having that film done. You had to wear the same clothes every day of course, and everything had to be exactly the same as it was the day before. If you had a bow it had to be the same, and your hat, if it was to one side it had to be the same. It was quite an excitement that was.

Sarah Ann Evans

We'd go down to Minsterley on a bus and get dolled up in all these clothes, and then we'd come back up. We'd have to spend a lot of time waiting about, you'd have to wait 'til the sun came out before they could film. I was in the baptism scene as well. I should think we were there for the biggest part of August. We were paid thirty shillings a day – that was a lot of money that was – we thought we were in clover ! But we had to take our own sandwiches, and we ate them in the chapel.

Doreen Rowson

Local tradesmen were also in demand.

It was a great occasion, everyone was happy seeing the village mentioned in the paper. Mr Williams the builder had the job of putting Lordshill chapel ready for filming. I was a joiner and had the job of making the porches. There was two porches, one very fancy on the front and one on the side. The porch is still there, surprising how it's kept over the years. When they were filming they asked us to go up, in case anything needed to be altered suddenly. The day before they started filming they realised they hadn't got any toilets, so we had to work all through the day and up until midnight making these toilets. They were only buckets, but we had to build them from scratch. Mr Williams used to own the grocer's shop and the building firm, and wouldn't miss a chance of making money, and put a sign in the shop window, 'Jennifer Jones' knickers for sale'. I don't know where he got them from! I remember the Condover Band going

Some of the cast of "Gone to Earth"
From left: Beatty Jones, Silvia Jones, Mavis France, Walton Humphrey, Lydia Harrison, Doreen Rowson, Betty Davies, Terence and Ken Jones

down to just below the chapel and playing. The film people were very friendly, they'd come and chat to you when they weren't acting. We had to build a baptismal chamber twice where Jennifer Jones was baptised. The first one they planned to do in a farmer's field, but he wanted about £300 for it, and that was a lot of money in those days, so instead of paying him £300 they built another in a different place near the chapel. My father helped build that. The actors and actresses got changed at Minsterley Parish Hall and they'd go up on a bus. They needed a lot of floodlights for the filming, so they had to put the generator over the hill in the other valley to reduce the noise. It was summer time and the film company were here for about a month. I remember we had to try and cover all the sheet iron up that was on any building, we had to camouflage it with paint.

John Francis

When they filmed Gone to Earth we moved the scenery around and the props and the tackle. Bill Price used to take it all around on our low-loader.

Ethel Tomlins

The Lordshill chapel choir took part in the film, but there were mixed feelings about it.

Dad didn't want it. "No", he said, "You should not do it in the place of worship." Some people reckoned they had a lot of money for the chapel, but they didn't have a penny. Some of the members started grumbling after, but dad said, "It's no good you grumbling, we had the meeting about it, you should've spoke out then, so it's no good you grumbling." Dad didn't want it, he said, "It's no place for a film."

Peggy Chidley

7: For richer, for poorer

Gatten Lodge, former home of the Hulton-Harrop family

Two World Wars changed the economic face of Britain for ever and nowadays the early years of the century are often portrayed in simplistic terms of two polarised classes. The image of 'the rich man in his castle, the poor man at his gate' has persisted, so that it is possible to believe that communities consisted solely of the Squire and his family on the one hand and a host of peasants serving their needs on the other! Extremes of both wealth and poverty were, of course, prevalent everywhere. The relationship between the different groups, however, seems to have been much more complex than might at first appear.

In particular, a strong element of inter-dependence between, for example, local land owners and their tenants and workers emerges. On the Stiperstones this is nicely exemplified by the situation of mining families who came to the area for work and built their own cottages on the rocky hillside claiming 'squatters' rights'. This was a situation which, as is indicated in Mr R Hulton-Harrop's account, the landowners tolerated because it brought them benefits. There was a circle of dependence therefore, though the balance of power was certainly not equal. In the days before tenants' rights were enshrined in law, there were many stories of evictions and high-handed action by landowners. Alongside them, however, can be told tales of paternalistic care and acts of unexpected kindness.

Generally speaking, large families were the rule of the day and, at a time when wages were often low (even in relative terms) and employment protection unheard of, many people lived – literally – 'on the bread-line'. Life was centred round the need to eat and keep a roof over your head, and a fear of the workhouse and parish relief lingered long into the 20th century. Money was earned in whatever way came to hand and the seasons and the rhythm of the farming year were important factors in economic survival. On the Stiperstones, the whinberry 'harvest' provided a vital opportunity for the whole family to help enhance the family coffers. The slow and meticulous task of picking these small dark berries features in almost everyone's recollections. Often, however, the memory is not an entirely happy one!

The squire had his hounds. I followed him to open the gate.

The Hulton-Harrop family owned a large swathe of land on the Stiperstones at one time. Here, Mr R Hulton-Harrop recalls the role his family played in the life of the local community and the relationships they had with the miners and farmers who occupied the land they owned.

Most landowners had a close relationship with their tenants. It was a case of live and let live. People do not realise how isolated this area was, access to the local market was a day's journey. Some people never left the area, tied to their farms all their lives, quite a few never saw the sea or visited London. The odd visit to Ludlow or Shrewsbury would have been the limit, with the local market a window on the world.

When minerals were discovered quite naturally we took advantage, taking a percentage of money from the minerals raised. However you get nothing for nothing. To get the minerals you needed miners and they needed somewhere to live with their families. Small settlement areas grew up on any corner of ground available that was not being used, often on the considerable areas of common land. As the mines were worked out, many of the small settlements were abandoned, returning to the soil. Others were sold to the occupiers, who settled permanently in the area. There was plenty of space and the land was not worth a lot in those days. The isolated nature of the area and general lack of employment controlled the permanency of the housing. There were disputes over land boundaries, but often the cost of litigation to prove ownership was simply not worth the value of the land being argued over, so we would let it go.

Land was given to the miners to build their homes but the land was of little use as agricultural land. It was in poor condition, in open or steep positions which made farming difficult, very little yield came from this land. The Harrop family, for these reasons, gave the land at Blakemoorgate to the miners because as landowners they were to earn more money from the mines than from the land. The miners needed somewhere to live so that the family could make a profit from the land. We had very little to do with the min-

ing communities, they were the responsibility of the mine operatives.

From an interview with R Hulton-Harrop.

Originally, there was a system that allowed you to continue building if you could get smoke through the chimney in such a time. We lived at Gittinshaye up on the Gatten. Old Squire Harrop took the roofs off the places when the folks went out or died because we were only squatters.

Johnny Butler

Squatter's cottage at Blakemoregate.

The squire had his hounds. I followed them to open the gates. You would doff your cap, always did that and the squire might chuck you a couple of bob and you'd clear off sharpish and look after it. The squire was well respected, he was quite decent really.

Jack Pugh

There was pheasant and grouse shooting days. The shooters would have their lunch at the keeper's cottage – well that was us – when they cleared off me and our Mary ate the 'horts' (left overs). The only time I ever knew what horseradish was.

Johnny Butler

Hulton-Harrop would go round and tell the whinberry pickers to keep off the hill on the day of the grouse shoot, there'd be about eight guns. There were stone butts for the guns. It was great it was. I used to go beating for Hulton-Harrop on the Stiperstones and then when I was fifteen I went to The Long Mynd with Mr Humphrey. There was a lot of grouse on the Stiperstones then, there was plenty on the Long Mynd as well. We had setter trials up there, (trials of setter dogs which were used to find and 'set' or 'point' grouse by their scent for shooting purposes; such trials can only be held when grouse are numerous). *You could drive grouse easily on the Stiperstones. We could make up four or five good drives. You can drive grouse with the wind in the morning but in the afternoon you have to bring them back into the wind because they have to go back where they came from.*

There was some rough shooting over at Nipstone but that was a syndicate.

Henry Owen

I remember them shooting the grouse on the hill. We weren't allowed on the hill on those days especially to pick whinberries.

Doris Hewitt

In the bad winter of 1947 there was grouse all under the rocks, hundreds of them there were and there was nothing for them to eat. We thought we'd creep up on them with a .410 but they heard us.

Wilfred Andrews

I remember when I was a kid I found a grouse's nest at the top of Wardmans Hollow and I touched the eggs and that grouse forsook her nest.

Doris Hewitt

In the days before the Welfare State, National Insurance and unemployment benefit, responsibility for provision for the needy rested with each parish. Elsie Rowson remembers a story, passed down through generations of her husband's family, about 'Parish Pay' and how strictly the rules surrounding it were applied.

I remember me mother-in-law telling me how poor her mother was. She was left a miner's widow. She was left with one son and seven daughters and she used to take in washing. Her only pay was two shillings a week, which she had to go to Hope to collect from Parish Pay, and there was her and a Mrs Priscilla Preece – she lived up the Dingle – and they used to go together to collect their two shillings from the Rectory at Hope. One day Mrs Priscilla Preece said could she bring her two shillings, because one of the children was very poorly with measles and so Granny Dyas went to Hope, and when she got there they said if she couldn't collect it herself she wasn't entitled to it. So Granny Dyas ran all the way from Hope over the fields, Hogstow Hall and up to Mrs Priscilla Preece's and stayed with the child while Mrs Priscilla Preece ran all the way back.

She'd got to get back there before they closed the books, because if they closed the books she didn't get it.

Elsie Rowson

The spectre and reality of the workhouse was still very much alive in the years before the Second World War.

The farmer fetched this lad from the workhouse. There was muck up to your flippin' knees 'cos there was no road as such, only ruts, like, and he'd be stood up in the cart with his fancy top stockings and these breeches, and this little owd nipper would be struggling leading the horse through the muck. "C'mon boy", he'd say. He was probably illegitimate or something. It was a terrible system, it was in the 1930s, after the General Strike and the slump, and things was as bad as they ever would be.

Johnny Butler

'Dole', or unemployment benefit, was paid out during the depression years from a building, still standing, in Minsterley opposite the meat canning factory in Station Road. However, payment was subject to a strict 'means test'.

At one time my father couldn't get dole 'cos he got a few sheep and cattle, so they gave him three days on the road and he had 15 shillings to keep four children. They were hard days.

Les Hotchkiss

There used to be dole in them days. You had to walk to Minsterley to sign on. They used to have what you call the 'means test', and if you'd got a cow and you were on the dole, they wouldna allow you nothing. You'd got to sell your cow. One bloke they went to see and he'd got a piano there and they said, "Is that your piano?" "Yes", he said. "We canna give you no dole 'til you've sold your piano", they said.

Gordon Cook

The dole office was in Minsterley, and there'd be a gang of blokes from there to the Creamery, they went down there twice a week – once to sign on and the next to draw their two or three shillings, like, whatever it was. But if they'd got stock, like, an old cow or anything, then they'd dock so much off your dole money – it was a poor old existence.

And for some of them they only got as far as the Bath Arms or the Bridge, or the Miners Arms, as they called it in them days, so there was very little ever went home, and it was hard going.

Johnny Butler

At a time when there wasn't always a lot to go round, what little there was would often be readily shared.

I remember a boy starting at Huglith, he pulled his bait out of this awd rag he'd got it tied up in, and all he'd got was a piece of dried bread and a kipper for his lunch to take him through the day. We shared our lunch with him for a week until he got his money as he could buy summat.

Heber Rowson

Tramps were a common sight on the roads of rural England in the 1920s and '30s.

The tramps would travel, have a meal and a wash, work in the garden for a while until they'd paid for what they'd have then they would put on their coats and go off to the next one.

Margaret Buckley-Atkins

I remember tramps coming round tramping from workhouse to workhouse. Stone House at Bishops Castle was a workhouse. They'd call at the farm and ask us to brew some tea for them. They had a tin can with a wire handle to it and they'd ask mum to boil some water for them and they might ask if they could stop the night in the barn. Dad was always very kind to the tramps, he used to take them a basin of bread and milk out at a night just before they went to bed, and they'd have gone by the time we got up in the morning and you'd never see anything else of them. He'd say they could stop there as long as they liked, as long as they didn't smoke. He was afraid of a fire in the hay.

John Francis

Families of Romany gypsies were also regular visitors, plying their trade and using skills handed down over many generations to earn some money, and then moving on.

Gypsies stayed in the stack yard at the farm. There were three or four gypsy caravans parked there, with piebald horses with their legs tied together. They were true gypsies, eating hedgehogs and rats, selling pegs and flowers made from woodshavings. They'd buy rabbit skins and feathers from chickens, ducks and geese, for quilts and eiderdowns. They could put a curse on you. You was always frittened of the curse.

Doug Boulter

The gypsies would park up on the wasteland. One child was born under a tree in our field, my dad was a methodist and offered to christen it. He christened her Hazel because the mother hadn't got a name for her. They would stay a while and then they'd move on, nobody minded them somehow. They wouldn't be able to steal much. The women would sell pegs or tell your fortune, one gypsy man would come and see dad and out would come the fiddles and they'd have a little tune.

Margaret Buckley-Atkins

Gypsies would come to the pool [The Gravels] to peg make using the willows. They'd travel through for the 'hopping' at Tenbury Wells. Dad, being the postman, would write their letters for them. They burnt Granny Lock's 'van and all her belongings on the Grit when she died. They'd go whinberrying on the Long Mynd on flat carts and sometimes the women would have a real 'set-to' and the blokes would never say a word.

Jim Booth

Before the Second World War tinkers you knew came around the farms, they'd buy rabbit skins and sell clothes pegs. We would get a little old chap coming round with a donkey and cart collecting scrap. He'd have rock salt and you'd barter with him, an old grate for some rock salt for the cattle.

Jack Pugh

Every so often we would get Tickney Bennett from Pontesbury come round with a little old donkey and a flat cart. He would be after rags, bones and rabbit skins. He would also be selling all kinds of crockery and rock salt for the animals.

From "Recalling the Past" by George Evans

You'd go to Shrewsbury perhaps twice in the year

You'd go to Shrewsbury perhaps twice in the year. You wouldn't go oftener than that, not from The Bog we wouldn't, we never did. Well you didn't have the money to spend for a start and then there was the journey! You'd go to buy some clothes or shoes.

Sarah Ann Evans

Travelling salesmen played a vital role in remote rural communities by bringing the goods needed for everyday life to the doorsteps of their customers.

Mr Walton used to come round every month. He lived up The Mount in Shrewsbury. He was a tailor. He used to sell clothes. Mum used to buy things for us, especially for anniversaries. Clothes were always bought off him and payment was spread out over perhaps nine months or twelve months. He used to come every month to collect the money. Anniversary times were so special, we had a new dress or a new coat. We used to pick whinberries to pay for the anniversary clothes.

Ruth Chesters

The Hotchkiss family at Coldhill, The Bog.

Charley Brown, 'Charley the packman' most people called him, used to come every eight weeks. He sold shirts, socks and stockings. He carried them in a very neat pack on his back wrapped up in what we used to call oil cloth. There also came another man we called 'The six week man'. He carried his stuff in a wooden box with leather straps on it, to go over his shoulders. He sold reels of cotton, needles, razors, scissors and spectacles with steel rims. Once or twice a year, Morris the tin man would come around. He dealt in dairy utensils, milk buckets, milk pans and all the things for the dairy and butter making. He would be selling new things but would also mend things at the same time, such as soldering things. If it was a big job he would take it with him and bring it back next time round like new.

From "Recalling the Past" by George Evans

'Make do and mend' was the order of the day and footwear in particular – being a relatively costly item – had to be made to last.

You had one pair of Goodyear boots to last twelve months from Tom Parry Central Stores, hob nailed. You had a square piece of leather from Toby Challinor's to mend the boots to make 'em last. Best clothes – you'd put 'em on and when you came back from wherever you'd take 'em off and put the owd clobber back on.

Heber Rowson

We very rarely went to Shrewsbury. Dad used to get our boots from Parry's at Central Stores. But you only had one pair in twelve months. He repaired them, mended his own boots. He'd buy leather, then you could buy it in strips. He used to cut it out, the shape of the boot and put it on with little tack pins, they called sprigs.

Johnny Roberts

I had a hole in the bottom of my shoe and I can remember cutting cardboard socks to put in the bottom of my shoe 'til mum could get to Shrewsbury to buy me a new pair and then when she did – they always just bought one size bigger than what you'd had before. Well I must have grown a lot 'cos I could have done with two sizes bigger. She brought 'em home, we were going on a school trip the next day. So I put these shoes on and I thought they're a bit tight, but I had to wear them because I couldn't have gone on the trip

if I hadn't. I spent half the day with them off my feet an the trip 'cos they were too tight and did I get a belting for that because I'd spoiled the shoes and she couldn't take them back and they never were any good.

Millie Gough

There were folks with patches on their behinds in them days. I expect that it was a hallmark that you'd got a good mother if you'd got a patch on your behind!

Jack Pugh

Not a scrap of food would be allowed to go to waste.

Us kids would come home from school and her'd put us our tea and if we'd bought any bits back, 'cos there was no school meals in those days, her'd eat them 'horts' [left overs] while we ate our tea.

Johnny Butler

There was a family nearby who were very poor. When the children came home from school their meal would consist of a piece of dry bread and a cup of tea with one spoonful of brown sugar. They were not allowed to stir the tea. The piece of bread would be divided, with one piece being eaten with the cup of tea, and on the other they were allowed to spread the brown sugar from the bottom of the tea cup. And that was their meal.

Emily Griffiths

There was a fishman that would come up from Pontesbury and his name was Mr Gough. He called at granny's just as grandad had got home and handed over the wage packet. The fishman said to granny, "Is that all you've got to manage on?", and she said, "Yes." He told her, "Fetch me a bowl", so she fetched him a bowl and he filled it full of herrings for her. He said, "I don't know how you manage with all these kids and on that much." (Susie's grandmother had given birth to as many as twenty-one children although not all survived.)

Susie Hartshorn

Anything for a penny in those days

My mum worked all her life. She worked at the Hall Farm in Minsterley for nine years. She could feather a fowl, she could make hay, she could make butter. She could do anything. She used to feather fowl for people for sixpence a time, anything for a penny in those days.

Mollie Rowson

Anything for which there was a ready market would be gathered and sold.

Mum and dad would gather moss up on Rhadley, fill sacks of moss, they used to supply Murrell's, Weaver's and Nichols' with moss. They would go twice a week to Shrewsbury with moss because in those days funeral wreaths were made with wreath frames and moss.

Betty Hordley

The down from the geese was kept separate for eiderdowns, but the wing feathers, you'd sell those, the whole wing for dusting.

Jack Pugh

A lot of people lived on rabbit, especially the big families. The skins would be dried and hung up, then sold to people that came round, and mole skins, I've sold hundreds. I used to go mole trapping when I was at school, get the skins and nail them to the back of the building door. I'd get 20-30 skins and send them away to Wisbech.

Henry Owen

I was making more money at home on rabbits than I was by going to work. The fields was walking with them. We had rabbitting dogs – two hounds and a little lurcher. I'd rear ferrets and sell them at a pound a piece. There was always lots of ways in them days for making a fair bit of extra money.

Wilfred Andrews

What would now be called 'flexible working patterns' were commonplace as people sought any way they could to bolster their incomes.

They used to do anything to get a bit extra. My dad and my Uncle George would go round mowing with scythes for five bob an acre.

Les Hotchkiss

You'd go and help on the farms in the evening or go rabbitting or shooting for a bit of extra money for wine, women and song!

Jim Harper

The oldest holly trees were at the Vessons. John Hayward cut the holly and wrapped it into bundles with a bit of berry to put on the top. It went to Manchester on the Sunday and Monday coming up to Christmas. You could get 10 shillings a week for cutting holly. I was about twelve years old.

Doug Boulter

The money wasn't about like it is now. I seen the time, when I was smoking, when Woodbines was 2d for five and 4d for ten, and I'd be fishing around for a packet of fags. That was when I was about eighteen or nineteen, and I remember we had some walnut trees at home and I picked these walnuts, the state of my hands they was green, I'd got some gloves on but it came through. I took 'em up to Middletown pub, Charlie Pugh was there and he gave me a shilling a pound for them, and I thought that's great that is! Yet folks, they lived, they made do, they didn't go out, they'd got nothing to go out with!

George Balmer

We sawed logs, we fetched birch trees and I sawed them with a cross-cut saw with my sister to save the coal.

Heber Rowson

An occasional stroke of luck or an unexpected act of kindness would stay long in the memory.

Joe was working at Malehurst when we got married and his wages was two pound ten shillings and we paid Mrs Rowson ten shillings a week for rent – so we did everything else out of two pounds. He had very little pocket money and I remember once, one Friday, doing some extra washing, and I was washing some old trousers and I pulled the pocket out to rub it and out came a ten bob note folded up in a square. I pegged it on the line in the sun and dried it, and every few minutes I kept going outside to see the wind hadn't blown it away. I tell you what, that was a find.

Elsie Rowson

The biggest milk cheque we had was six pound a month, and one day me dad lost it. We 'adna got no money and the local people did a bit of a collection and give us a bit of money to carry on. Them was good days then, wanna they?

Gordon Cook

Money wasn't always spent 'wisely', but small pleasures in what could be a remorselessly hard life were relished.

One of the miners used to live with his aged parents right up the top of the Dingle. He'd be working a seven 'til three shift and he'd come in soaked to the skin from Huglith mines. He would drink like a fish and smoke like a chimney. He told me once he got nine pounds a week, and that was 1938, when bank managers wouldn't be getting anywhere near that amount. Three pound was a good wage then. He'd spend £4 in the pub and give his parents £5. Four pounds was a fortune because you could buy ten Woodbines for 4d and a pint of Southams beer for 6d. He used to literally live in the pub. He survived until he was sixty which was extremly old for someone with silicosis.

Walton Humphrey

The annual Farmers' Ball at Minsterley was eagerly anticipated and long remembered.

I went to Minsterley Ball. It was a farmers do every year. I was a smart chap, I had a morning suit and a dickie bow tie, the trousers were striped, the jacket was black and a white shirt and a white hankerchief and the girls had long dresses.

George Balmer

Mum and dad used to go to the Farmers' Ball in the Parish Hall at Minsterley. It was the big ball of the year. Mother used to have a new dress.

Della Pugh

Della Pugh grew up at Snailbeach Farm at a time when their ownership of a telephone was a considerable novelty, but one that was readily shared.

We had the only telephone in the village for many, many years, I think I was about four when they put it in. Everybody knew about this telephone and they came to use it. It was number 5, Minsterley. If anyone came for the doctor – Dr. Jameson – he used to call for my father to go with him to tell him where the houses were. On horseback they used to set off all hours of the day and night. Mother and dad never minded anybody coming to use the phone. Mr O'Grady, who lived at Prospect House, used to court the daughter from Jones, the Hurst Farm, everyday he used to come to telephone and leave 2d on the table for the call. The telephone was like a box that was on the wall with a hand set that was hung on it, but it had like accumulators in it. It was a big thing to have, a telephone. There was no exchange, only the Minsterley Post Office. We went to school with the Roberts' who kept Minsterley Post Office. The older ones were friends with my elder sisters, and they used to talk about gramophone records, and if anyone had a new record they'd play it down the phone and the others would play one back.

Della Pugh

At the Stiperstones Inn, Walton Humphrey remembered a life which had its moments of excess but which also depended on keeping the bank manager 'sweet'.

At the end of the season my mother and my sister would go and have a big spend up, and they'd go into Shrewsbury and mother would open her bag up – it was like a doctor's bag and there'd be stacks of pound notes in there and they'd go to Della Porta's and Winnie would have a fur coat when fur coats were fur coats!

My father was always into big money and big thinking – it didn't worry him. At times he would literally have no money, he'd be working on an overdraft. He once had an overdraft of £200, well it might as well have been a million 'cos he hadn't got it! He always used to have the garden done beautifully and you'd see Mr Hughes, the bank manager from the Midland in those days, he would make a trip out to see him. My father would entertain him and have his best tweeds on and take him round the garden to simmer him down a bit. Then in the end it would come right.

Walton Humphrey

They'd say we'd have to pick our clothes off the hill

With the end of the hay harvest another harvest began as families took to the hillside to pick the crop of whinberries that grow on the heather-clad sides of the Stiperstones. This painstaking harvest was essential, it brought in extra money to families that were already poverty striken through the fluctuation of the miners' wages.

The whinberries were mostly used for dyes, they ripened in early July and continued until the first early frosts of Autumn. School holidays, usually six weeks, coincided with this crop. Whole families spent all of their available time picking for as little as three halfpence a quart [one and a half pounds].

Buyers, known locally as 'higglers', collected with a horse and cart. The ripe fruit was packed into small round wicker hampers, known as 'wiskets', which were lined with newspaper and taken for despatch to Minsterley Station. People would come rushing down the hillsides when they heard a hand-bell rung, or the higgler's shout, "Now for 'em!"

The extra cash would eke out a meagre budget by helping to buy a load of coal for winter, a pig for fattening up, new boots for the children going back to school, yarn for home knitting, material for clothes and any number of other needs.

Emily Griffiths

We'd go whinberrying and cranberrying up by the Devil's Chair. (The cranberry is a red berry similar in size to the whinberry but much sharper in flavour. Flower books refer to them respectively as bilberry and cowberry. The cowberry, though common on the Stiperstones is seen virtually nowhere else in Shropshire.) I'd go with my mum and sister until I left school. We'd put some stones out and have a little fire and cook bacon on a little fork and have a picnic. It was right nice. They'd say we'd have to pick our clothes off the hill – pick whinberries to sell to buy clothes to go back to school.

Wilfred Andrews

The extra money earned was an essential part of each family's income and used for a wide variety of purposes.

If you was very fortunate to pick whinberries on the hill and get some money, you might go to Minsterley Show!

My mum was seven years old when her dad died and they picked whinberries every year to buy a pig and to buy their boots for twelve months.

Mollie Rowson

We used to have to pick whinberries all our summer holidays, we were always up on the hill. Jack Wardman would come up from Snailbeach shouting for whinberries and the people would come down off the hill with them. We'd get about 6d a quart. I wasn't a very good picker, I was from the town. If I could get two quarts that was good. The money would go towards clothes, rent or buying the next pig. Some people would come from The Gravels with a great big market basket and they would fill that! Jim Jones who lived at The Rock used to make the rent by picking whinberries.

Sarah Ann Evans

We picked whinberries in a National Dried Milk tin and we sold them for 5d a pound. The hill would be covered with people, they'd come walking up the railway line in droves at nine o'clock in the morning from Pontesbury.

Doug Boulter

We had no option but to go whinberry picking, we went, gangs of us, some would come up from Pontesbury. We would get a few heather stalks together and light a fire to make a tin of tea, we'd get over into the fields and catch old Cook's cow and pinch a bit of milk.

At the end of the summer before you went back to school you'd get taken to Salop [Shrewsbury] to get a pair of boots.

Johnny Butler

Picking the whinberries without including a fair number of the tiny green leaves also was a difficult, almost impossible, task. However, there were quick methods of separating the two.

I have a mind's eye picture still of Mrs Hotchkiss on a clear and windy day in the farmyard outside the kitchen with her four lovely children holding between them at all four corners, a sheet. Their mother held above it in turn the basket and buckets of bilberries and poured them into the sheet. This was real winnowing, allowing the wind to blow away the loose whinberry leaves and chaff, to leave the berries as clean as possible for market.

From "The Rock" by Jeanette Merry

We used to go to the hill every day during the six weeks summer holidays. George Williams who used to live at the Stiperstones took a lorry to The Long Mynd with people and baskets and back at night. We'd clean the whinberries quickly by sitting outside with the whinberries on a tray and blowing the leaves off. You would take them to Wardman's shop where Ben Wardman used to come. He would weigh them with your basket and then he would weigh the basket when it was empty and deduct it. We had new shoes to go back to school with the money. We'd play a bit on the hill. I was never a very quick picker.

Ruth Chesters

Whinberries, also known as bilberries

George Williams from Perkins Beach transported villagers to The Long Mynd for the whinberry picking at sixpence a trip. That was a great day out – to get water from the Boiling Well and brew up over a heather stalk fire. It was a village day out because it was a big income in those days whinberry picking.

Mrs Lewis from Gorsty Bank would come round on a horse and trap driven by her son calling at various points around the village to pick up whinberries. She'd pull out her little leather pouch and pay you as she weighed them. She would take them down to Minsterley Station where they went to the dye factories.

Derek Rowson

Granny would go whinberry picking with a big old umbrella and all the children. If it rained they thought they'd be going back home but " Oh no! Come and get here under the 'yeth' [heather]. She'd put this great big umbrella up and all these kids would scuttle underneath it. "Get under me apron", she'd say if it was only to be a shower and it would dry up and they'd go on picking.

Susie Hartshorn

"They'd say we'd have to pick our clothes off the hill"

There was a certain amount of fun to be had on the hillside – particularly for children – and an element of companionship, but the hard, relentless task of actually picking the whinberries is often remembered with mixed emotions.

My mother was one of twelve children and they all had to pick whinberries. We had to pick whinberries as well. You'd get your school holidays and that's where most of it was spent. I hated whinberry picking, you never got a wet day them summers.

Les Hotchkiss

I used to go whinberry picking but I hated it! I used to pray for rain. When I went up the Dingle onto the hill I could see Corndon Hill, if he had got his cap on it might rain. I couldn't bear whinberrying but I went! It was alright on the hill, the worst part was picking whinberries, I'd have a chat to the Pontesbury folks or anybody that came along. I didna like blackberrying either, they scratches you!

Dolly Harrison

Corndon 'had got his cap on' when the summit was covered in low-lying cloud.

I went once and counted my whinberries 2,218!

Della Pugh

I loved picking whinberries, Emily Griffiths found a whinberry crossed with a cranberry once and brought it to Girl Guides. Up Silfords Hollow, up on the rocks, there used to be a patch of white whinberries. We picked blackberries for 1d a pound. We'd pick bucketfuls, seventy years ago they were very plentiful.

Doris Hewitt

WHINBERRYING BY THE DEVIL'S CHAIR

I've got none, and you've got none, we'll start as we mean to go on.

Young couples often began their married lives with virtually nothing between them – but at least that ensured they were on equal footing and prepared them for a life of penury.

My Uncle Tom and Aunty Florrie got married at Marton Chapel and they must have gone by horse and trap and on their way back coming over Whinberry Top [on the Farm Lane up to Snailbeach] he looked at her and he said, "How much have you got in your pocket owd mate?", I think it was a threepenny bit or a sixpence, I'm not sure which, and he said, "Right, chuck it over the hedge", and they did so. "There", he said, "I've got none and you've got none we'll start as we mean to go on", and that's what he did on Whinberry Top, throwed their last bit of silver over the hedge. It's most probably there now.

Nellie Rowson

The larger families suffered in those days. It was difficult to feed a big family, there was hard times for quite a few families. Even so in that era each and everyone was an equal. It didn't matter for those who were poor, everybody still associated with everybody else.

Graham France

Nobody treated anybody as if they were poor. I said to Emily [Griffiths] one day, "I never felt I was poor did you?", and she said, "No, but we were".   Margaret Buckley-Atkins

In the diaries he kept towards the end of his long life, Bill Francis described in stark and dramatic terms the level of real poverty endured at one time by many hill farmers on the Stiperstones and elsewhere.

30th August 1985

As I sit here surrounded by semi-luxury all and more of my needs supplied, complaining of my failing strength and contemplating the start of my 90th winter on this earth, I ponder a while on what life would have been like in that first winter of 1896. A husband who had to be at the pit head for 6 am to descend into the bowels of the earth to earn the meagre wages paid at that time; sheep and cattle to feed, clean and milk often in driving, drifting snow; three squawking daughters aged three years, five and seven or eight, a complaining granny and lastly, myself – no doubt a puny babe of six months or so whimpering to suck at breasts half the time dry through poverty. I know I was breast fed. She told me often in later life that she believed in the adage that it was preferable to feed one child over long at the breast than carry another in the womb.

Merciful God, if I were placed in her situation I'm afraid I should contemplate mass murder and suicide. Small wonder she died worn out at sixty-nine.

From the diaries of Bill Francis

8: In sickness and in health

The Nurse's Bungalow

"I should not like to say much more than 50 or 55 years". This was the answer given by Dr John Hughes of Worthen when questioned in 1863 by Lord Kinnaird and other members of the Mines Commission about the life expectancy of Stiperstones miners. The high mortality rate resulted partly from the prevalence of accidents in the mines and partly from respiratory and other diseases caused by their working conditions. Poor housing and a limited diet were also major contributory factors. Virulent epidemics could also sweep through communities with devastating effect, sometimes claiming the lives of a whole generation of a family.

In later years, the professional health care provided 'round the clock' by the District Nurse was much appreciated in country areas. The local GP, however, was often seen as distant physically and beyond the pocket of many people. In such circumstances, quaint and sometimes bizarre homespun remedies were regularly resorted to. Often these remedies had been used over many generations. Whether it was a piece of bacon fat hung around the neck or a shallot in the ear, their strength lay in the faith people invested in them.

Before the establishment of the National Health Service and the Social Security system as we know it today, care of the sick and elderly relied largely on local organisations, Friendly Societies and the goodwill of families, friends and neighbours.

No National Health Service or Workmen's Compensation Scheme existed in the Snailbeach Mine's heyday. The only form of support, apart from the dreaded Parish Relief [the Workhouse], was a voluntary organisation known as a Friendly Society. These had titles such as 'The Oddfellows' or 'The Ancient Order of Foresters', which were the two most popular in this area. Members paid a subscription which entitled them to a small benefit should they be ill or injured and some compensation for widows and orphans.

Emily Griffiths

The services of a doctor were not always accessible.

Well you'd got to be very ill before you had a doctor, because you couldn't afford to have one. No, very seldom you had a doctor.
                                                    Gordon Cook

And to gain admission to a hospital was also far from being straight forward.

If people wanted to get into hospital they'd have to have a recommendation to go from perhaps a parson or a baronet or someone like that. They would be allowed so many recommendations, you couldn't go to hospital on a doctor's say so without getting one of these certificates of recommendation. I think when I had to go into hospital to have my tonsils out when I was three, Sir Offley Wakeman supplied the recommendation.
                                                    Emily Griffths

You had to have a recommendation from someone of local standing to go into hospital. The vicar or someone like that had to say you were in need of hospital care. I went to see my mother in hospital, they were very strict in those days at the old Royal Salop Infirmary in Shrewsbury.
                                                    Jack Pugh

Medical and dental treatment could lack some of the sophistication we now take for granted.

The dentist used to come to school and you would go in thinking, "Am I for it or not?", and they would pull these teeth out – no anesthetic! Your mouth would be nothing but blood. You had to go to the washbasin and spit it out. I remember poor Brian Evans he had three teeth out in one day. He had to go and just lean over the washbasin and let the blood run out. There was no sympathy for you!
                                                    Doug Boulter

For Mollie Rowson a childhood injury left lasting reminders.

When I was nine I broke my leg. I was off school for six months and I was in bed for a whole month in the kitchen and my splint was made by the carpenter Mr Fred Jones. I've got the mark of that splint today. I've had a corn round the back of my heel ever since. We had home-made crutches made by Mr Fred Jones.
                                                    Mollie Rowson

It was 6d a month for the nurse

In such a rural area the District Nurse was often the only source of professional health care available. On the Stiperstones, a District Nursing Association was formed in 1916 with the intention of establishing and funding the service. Money was collected through subscriptions and fund-raising events such as concerts, jumble sales, sports days and dances. Nurse Mary Hurst was the area's first District Nurse. When she married Mr Alfred Williams from Snailbeach in 1922, Nurse Charlotte Hand was appointed and she continued in the post until her death in 1953, aged sixty-eight. She lived from the late 1920s onwards in what is still known locally as the Nurse's Bungalow, in Snailbeach, a building erected and paid for by local effort.

Nurse Charlotte Hand, Local District Nurse for 31 years

The village had a nurse and we had to keep that nurse. We had little dances at The Bog. Dora Price collected 6d a month for the nurse, from Snailbeach to Kinnerton and Uncle Herbert collected a shilling a month for the doctor.

Mollie Rowson

The nurse was on call 24 hours a day, if you wanted a nurse you get on your bike and go down the road and knock her up, she'd come.

Roly Johnson

For Jack Pugh, living in Plox Green, the nurse lived a mile uphill at Snailbeach.

To fetch the nurse it was said you had to, "Run the dirty mile".

Jack Pugh

Nurse Hand would come to school and inspect your hair with this special comb to see if you'd got nits. You knew the poor kids who got the nits 'cos they were sent outside and down to the old stone washbasin and under the cold tap with a bit of disinfectant.

Doug Boulter

The nurse was on call
24 hours a day

that!" Nurse Williams said, only to be told, "You look after the little un and we'll look after the missus!"

There were four bigger children who had been under the bed the previous night, that was where they slept – she had never known that they had been there when she was delivering the baby!

Connie Read

Although the District Nurse was held in great esteem by the local people the choice of a career in nursing was not always looked upon with approval,

I wanted to go nursing and mother said to me, "I canna bear you to go nursing you'll be looking at naked men." She was a prude..........mother and her bare bodies, I laid out ninety-nine old men and women and then I stopped counting!

Margaret Buckley-Atkins

Nurse Williams could tell you some tales, she'd been retired all my life, but she'd been the District Nurse. She would probably have a delivery at one end of the hill and walk to the other end for another and might have to carry the water, and might have to gather the sticks to light the fire to get the hot water for her patient. She went to one place and said to the man, "Can you cope?", and he said he could manage everything except the butter. So thinking it would be a couple of pounds of butter from the house cow, she said, "I'll do the butter for you!". She found herself patting up forty pounds of butter! That was district nursing.

Someone had come to her at about half past two in the morning, "Would you come – the missus is having a babby?" So she went – it was a flat cart with a canvas top,they put a box for her to step on and she went in and delivered the child. She went back the next morning and mother was sitting up in bed with the bottom half of a cottage loaf with a fried egg on top of it. Of course in those days new mothers had gruel. "Oh she shouldn't be eating

For childbirth they never dreamt of going to hospital

Before the Second World War, midwifery services were also provided by local women who specialised in the work but who had not necessarily been formally trained.

My mother was thirty-six and she had me at home and she booked a private midwife. She lived at the Roundhill near us, but she was never there because she was always out. She used to go to Manchester and Liverpool, everywhere to deliver babies. You had to pay the midwife. Mother wrote her a letter and she came by train. My dad met her with a horse and cart at Minsterley Station. She arrived in time to deliver me. My sister was born quite quickly and she did not have to send for the midwife.

There was a handy woman who lived in a cottage nearby, Mrs. Purslow, and she came and delivered my sister because she came in a hurry.
Margaret Buckley-Atkins

Hannah Perkin was the midwife and when you had a baby you stayed in bed for fourteen days.
Mollie Rowson

Hannah lived in Perkins Beach, behind the Stiperstones village, and is well remembered locally for the service and care she provided. She died in the 1920s.

A shallot in the ear and a piece of bacon fat around the neck!

For ordinary, everyday ailments there were a host of homespun remedies at hand, often passed down over many generations, and no matter how far fetched they seemed, they obviously had a certain degree of success.

If the doctor's services were unaffordable and the problem of a delicate nature, a wise woman in the village could always be relied upon for a remedy or a recipe.

In her novel, *The Golden Arrow*, Mary Webb conjures up a vivid picture of the work of one such woman.

Nancy Corra lived at a hamlet half way down the ridge, at some distance from Lostwithin, called the Clays..... She knew her secrets – secrets that might have possibly cost her life and certainly would have gained her several years in prison – were safe. Yet they were spread over the countryside in the keeping of gypsies, wives of labourers, barmaids at small taverns on untravelled roads, women who tramped, pedlars and unmarried girls of all classes. Her acknowledged patients old folks with rheumatism, rickety children, field workers with a gnashed hand or whitlow, drunkards' wives with bodies covered with bruises, she prescribed for with surprising efficiency ; her cures were simple, often drastic, usually very sensible. But her real patients – those who made her income – came in the evening, closely shawled.......

Elsie Rowson remembers how her Great Grandmother probably provided the inspiration for the character of Nancy Corra.

The mounds that grew no grass. (the Dressing Floor at Snailbeach).

Mary Webb writes about the mounds that grew no grass and the lady behind, and she used to make these potions for these girls to get rid of their babies. Mum used to say, "That's Granny Jones, that's your Granny Jones", the lady that lived behind the mounds that grew no grass.

Children were given a weekly dose of Epsom Salts, castor oil or brimstone and treacle. Home-made remedies included gorse blossom tea, yarrow tea and a mixture of butter, sugar and vinegar for sore throats, feverfew for headaches, greater celandine sap for curing warts or a local person would be asked to 'charm' them away. Bathing with salt and water would prevent blood poisoning, and often did! Boils were treated with plasters of carbolic soap and brown sugar. An alternative was to fill a bottle with boiling water, pour this out and apply the steam filled bottle immediately with the rim over the boil. Very painful but very effective. Emily Griffiths

I got a blackthorn in me knee and it was in there for about six months. It come out in the end and how I got it out was, I grated some soap and some rough sugar and made a poultice and put it on it. It fetched it out in ten minutes.

I remember I had about seven boils on the back of me neck and I got one of these poultices and put it on the back of me neck and I'll tell you what, it gave me a bit of stick for over five minutes and it went easy and I took the bandage off and the soap stuff and it burst the lot. Johnny Roberts

If we had a bad throat mother used to get a piece of fat bacon, put it on a piece of paper and that's what we had around our neck. For coughs you took black treacle and bacon liquor. If you had a bad chest you would rub it well with goose fat.

Mum always used to put a shallot in the oven, get that warmed up and put that in your ear for earache.
Peggy Chidley

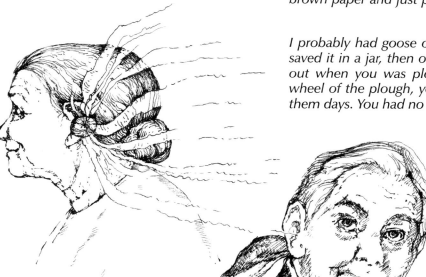

FIRST HEAT THE SHALLOT

BACON NECK TIE

If you had toothache you put pepper on it, and for a sore throat it was vinegar, butter and sugar. For a headache you had to get a dish, put some brown paper in it soaked in vinegar and put that on. Elsie Williams

For a bad chest it was tallow [candle wax] and brown paper. You had to warm the fat and put it on this brown paper and just put it on your chest.
Roly Johnson

I probably had goose oil rubbed on my chest, we saved it in a jar, then of course you'd take the rest out when you was ploughing and put it on the wheel of the plough, you always greased things in them days. You had no oil. You'd pull the wheel off a cart, grease it with goose grease and put the wheel back on.
Jack Pugh

Another widely recalled remedy recorded in the Shropshire Magazine for a sore throat was a sweaty, unwashed sock being tied around the neck. A remedy for goitre, a common ailment in mineral mining areas, was to put a live mole in a stocking and tie in around the affected neck. By the time the mole had died the goitre would have gone.

For warts a black snail was to be rubbed on the warts and then impaled on a blackthorn. As the snail dies and decomposes the warts would disappear. If it proved difficult to find a black snail an alternative was to cut an apple in half, eat one half, the other half to be rubbed on the warts and buried.

The cranberry [cowberry], which ripened later than the whinberry [bilberry], was picked from the hill and used more widely by the local people because there was little call for them for sale. A remarkable fruit, they could be bottled in just cold water. In the winter the water would by then be a lovely rich pink and was poured off to be sweetened with honey for a cold cure. The remaining berries would be utilised for tarts.

Emily Griffiths

Mollie Wardman used to have terrible nosebleeds, she was in her shop one day when a traveller [travelling salesman] was there, and she said to him, "Quick get them keys out of the door and put 'em down my back."

Bernard Millington

My grandfather, William Lewis, was born in 1873. He escaped certain death in the Snailbeach mine disaster in 1895, when he stepped out of the cage to be replaced by another man who was killed when the cage crashed down the shaft. He became known as the 'Shropshire Wizard'. He was famous for his healing powers, with patients coming from as far away as Birmingham.
  Joe Hotchkiss had got yellow jaundice, so his father Gilbert took him there to be cured. But on no account were you to say thank you or offer any payment, or his remedy wouldn't work.

Clifford Lewis

Whole generations of children could be wiped out!

Immunisation and vaccination have now largely eradicated the childhood killer epidemics, such as diphtheria and scarlet fever referred to in local records. Children between the ages of three and fifteen were generally more susceptible to scarlet fever. If they were weak and lacked a good diet, they were a prime candidate for the disease, if the fever could not be controlled they died. Whole generations of young children could be wiped out in a single visitation of diphtheria, as recorded in the Stiperstones area in the early 1870s.

My grandmother's first three children were boys and the eldest who was five started school at the Stiperstones in the year the school was built. And there was a terrrible scourge, they said it was scarlet fever but I should think it was something more virulent than that, probably diphtheria; but every small child in the area died and my grandmother lost her three little boys within a fortnight, there was the five year old, the two and a half year old and the baby, a few weeks old. There was only one child who recovered from that and her name was Asthenath Hodgkiss and afterwards she was a deaf mute for the rest of her days.

Emily Griffiths

Today, it is difficult to even begin to comprehend the horror endured by these parents, helplessly watching their children slowly choke to death as the swelling of the throat worsened and the airways finally closed.

My sister had diphtheria. It suffocates you. If you didn't have diphtheria you could be a carrier. They came and took swabs off us, they put a stick thing down your throat. There was an isolation ward at Monkmoor in Shrewsbury.

Johnny Butler

My granny had eighteen children but she buried two within a fortnight of each other with measles. Granny was expecting Uncle Harry at the time and her sister came from Manchester to look after her, bringing her little girl with her who'd got measles. These two little ones, one was two years old and the other was three, died within a fortnight. The *children dwindled down to ten but she had one or two still-born as well. I think originally she had twenty-one.*

Susie Hartshorn

Of all the diseases which were prevalent amongst the population, tuberculosis or TB was the greatest killer. Sometimes a person with the disease showed no outward symptoms, living a relatively full life, but spread the disease to those who had a lower immunity. The disease was spread by coughing and sneezing and so the damp air within mines, together with often overcrowded living conditions provided the perfect environment for the disease to spread. The visible signs were a general wasting away and weakness of the body and the coughing of blood (the graveyard cough). The disease was also called consumption. Treatment generally included sleeping in a flow of fresh air.

My cousin had TB and used to be at Shirlett [a sanatorium], when the war broke out she came home, and she slept in my bed. I can remember us walking up to the Gravels to catch the bus to the May Fair in Bishops Castle and her stopping at every stile and coughing her heart out with this TB on her lungs, yet she was sharing a bed with me. In the end she got so bad she had a hut in the garden in Minsterley and she died there.

Millie Gough

If anyone had TB they would have one of them shelters in the garden. There were like stable doors on them and they used to turn around. It was something to do with the air. They used to have their beds in them.

Roly Johnson

There was a family at The Bog, Garner was their name. They were all riddled with consumption, one died at sixteen.

Emily Griffiths

It was my job to scrub out the Houses of Parliament!

By modern standards living conditions were often primitive.

On a local farm the maid's first job every morning when the household got up was to de-flea the beds, by catching them in her fingers. There were a lot of vermin about, rats were around the buildings in droves.

Doug Boulter

The toilets were all the way down the bottom of the yard. Granny lived next door and we all went to the same toilet. It didn't matter how many were there, you all went to the same toilet at the bottom end of the yard! You had a candle in a jam jar and string on it. Down the yard you went in the dark before you went to bed, a trail down the yard.

Mollie Rowson

It used to be my job to scrub out the 'Houses of Parliament' – well that's where all the business was done! Every week I had to do it, from when I was seven, and it was my job also to cut up nice sized pieces of newspaper and hang them on a string behind the door. If we ever had any tissue paper wrapping, the tissue paper would be cut into squares and put in a box for visitors. My sister used to vex me because she would always use the tissue from the visitors' box!

There was a box of soil kept on the seat with a bit of quick lime in it as well, and if you used the toilet you sprinkled some of the soil in with a little shovel. Once a year the toilet would be emptied into a hole dug under the plum trees. And when someone said because of it, "We had plums like nobody's business". We always said, "We had plums like everybody's business!".

Emily Griffiths

We called our outside toilet the 'Thunder House'. The walls were eighteen inches thick.

Jack Pugh

There has been a good deal of illness amongst the men

The mining population are decidedly weak in the lungs and if I had a lot of miners to examine for a life assurance society, and a lot of agricultural labourers; my opinion is that the majority of the agricultural workers would be [have] better lives than the miners.

Mr. John Hughes of Worthen, a medical officer, July 1863.

In the 1860s a commission was appointed to inquire into mining conditions in Great Britain. An interview is recorded between Mr. William Eddowes of Pontesbury, a surgeon who had been practising in the area since 1835 and attended the Snailbeach miners. When asked about the miners' health the doctor reported that at the smelting works *there has been a good deal of illness amongst the men*, he believed this illness to be *lead colic*. He also reported that a number of miners in the area were affected by lead colic, especially those who worked down the Gravels Mine. The reason being...

..owing to the work being dusty; it is very loose, and there was a good deal of carbonate of lead found at that time in the mine. They either inhaled it or they took it in from their fingers when eating, and of course they have no means of washing themselves, or if they do wash themselves it is of course impregnated with lead.

Conditions below the surface contributed to a variety of pulmonary diseases. Air circulation and ventilation was not always good and often deteriorated as the mine deepened. At Snailbeach the principal workings were below the 252 yard level so the majority of miners were required to climb over a hundred fathoms by ladder on their way to and from their workplace, the ascending journey taking as long as one hour. Facilities for the miners were inadequate, the Miners' Dry was a simple, windowless room, with little heating except for a number of exposed pipes from the boiler room next door. There were no showers or proper means of washing and it was in this building that the miners changed from their dirty, wet and sweaty mining clothes. Blasting too was a necessary evil, it was costly and time consuming and as wages depended on the amount of ore produced the miners were always anxious to return to the site of blasting all too quickly, leaving themselves open to gunpowder smoke and copious levels of dust.

I never knew a grandfather, both my grandfathers were dead and gone, long before I came on the scene and they had both died with pulmonary complaints from the effects of the mines. All the old death certificates showed it as miner's phthisis.

Emily Griffiths

The Compressor House at Snailbeach built 1881

The Widow Maker

Technological developments had a tremendous impact on the mining community in this area. Traditional, labour-intensive mining methods made way for technology in mining machinery and equipment. The Compressed Air Drill was introduced to the Snailbeach Mine in the 1880s and was used extensively throughout the mines in this area, including Huglith Mine, until the 1940s. Its use caused an incurable disease called silicosis. Silicosis is a specific form of pneumoconiosis caused by the inhalation of particles of silica, silica being mostly found in quartz in rocks. Inhalation of the fine silica dust particles generated by the Compressed Air Drill was to cause the prolonged suffering and ultimate death of many miners and thus earned the drill the macabre name of 'The Widow Maker'.

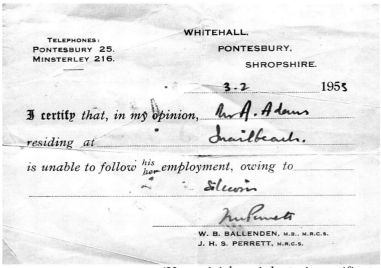

'Happy' Adams' doctor's certificate

'Happy' Adams at Huglith barytes mine with 'The Widow Maker'

Today there are many local people who can still remember the pain and suffering endured by family members and friends with silicosis, many of whom worked at Huglith Mine when it opened for barytes production in 1910.

My father had silicosis all the while I was growing up, his breathing was terrible. His heart gave way in the end with the strain. A lot of families in the village were affected. I never heard of men suffering in other mines like they did at Huglith.

Ruth Chesters

I was one year old when my father died and my eldest brother was fourteen. My father had been working down the mines for about fifteen years when he died. He was thirty-eight years old. He and another man called Elijah Parry were one of the first men to be diagnosed to have died from silicosis. The post mortem was held in the bedroom. What little compensation my mother got was kept by the County Court, and whenever she needed money, like to buy me my school clothes, she had to go before the judge in the public court and ask for it.

Arthur Davies

Elijah Parry had silicosis

My dad, Elijah Parry, had silicosis, he was really poorly and died at forty-five. It was no age, but when you saw him suffering you wished for the Lord to take him, he was gasping for his breath all the time. It was awful to be gasping for breath like that.

Dorothy Trow

My grandfather, Elijah Parry, was only forty-five years of age when he died in 1933 from silicosis. He was a very well-read man and he knew exactly what was wrong with him and without gran knowing he left his lungs to be examined to try to get compensation for other miners' families. When gran had to go to the inquest, his lungs were there in jars floating just like stones.

Phyllis Jones

My father was on the jury at Elijah Parry's inquest. They had to have an inquest, like a coroner's inquest on the man. I remember my father saying ever so well that the doctor said that this man had only got an area of lung about the size of a two shilling piece left to breath with, that's all. The rest was petrified, it almost like turned them into stone.

Emily Griffiths

Sadly, Mr Parry's widow received no compensation. The inquest did, however, help to establish the precedent and thereafter men with silicosis, and their families' were entitled to compensation.

Elijah Parry was only 45 when he died in 1933 of silicosis.

9: At the going down of the sun

"An incendiary came down right on the works"
The Snailbeach Works, Bonfire Night 1998

Although the main battlefields of both World Wars were many miles from the hills of South Shropshire, the people who lived on or around the Stiperstones were far from unaffected by the conflict.

Local young men were plucked from their families, friends and all they knew and cared for, and thrust into a harsh, even savage existence for which few were prepared. During the Second World War, others had to move to places like Birmingham and Wolverhampton to carry out jobs which were considered essential for the War effort, and some became 'Bevan Boys' working in the coal mines of South Wales and elsewhere. (All knew that a small part at least of their youthful naivety had been taken from them.)

Many recalled later that their Shropshire homes were never far from their minds, no matter where they travelled. They commented on the pleasure of an occasional meeting with someone from 'back home' and the chance to share stories and swap memories. The people they left behind did not forget them. Prayers were offered in the local churches and chapels for their safe return and fund-raising took place so that gifts could be sent to local lads who had been called-up.

At the same time, evacuees came to live in the area – bringing with them strange accents and different ways. The people of the Stiperstones opened their homes to these visitors as best they could. Some evacuees stayed to live here after the War had ended. Others kept in touch with friends they had made, and some still do so to this day.

A detachment of the Home Guard was formed locally and 'fire watch' patrols stayed awake at nights to keep a weather eye open for danger. And danger was never too far away. German bombers travelling to and from places like Liverpool and Manchester sometimes passed over the Stiperstones.

High-explosive bombs fell locally and on the never-to-be-forgotten night of the 9th April 1941 incendiary bombs rained down along the length of the Stiperstones from Snailbeach to The Bog.

The First World War 1914-1918

During the Great War of 1914-1918, prisoners of war were billetted locally. Their energies were put to good use by, amongst others, Colonel James Ramsden who owned and operated the Bog Mine at the time. P.O.W. labour was used to create and erect a six or seven mile long aerial rope-way running from the mine to the Malehurst barytes crushing mill between Pontesbury and Minsterley. Buckets of barytes travelling down to Malehurst and of coal travelling in the opposite direction were attached to a steel rope strung between wooden and metal pylons set in concrete bases. Some of the concrete bases of this impressive structure can still be seen in fields and on hillsides today.

The prisoners built the line for the aerial ropeway from The Bog to Malehurst

At first the Germans were quartered at the Midland Railway Yard at Coleham in Shrewsbury and travelled daily to Minsterley by train and then marched out under guard to the parts of the rope-way to be worked on. Later on, the prisoners were billetted at The Bog and supervision got more lax. We children got to know a lot of them by name. There was one, Paul Measler, I used to spend a lot of time with him. He had been a school teacher in Germany before the war. These chaps used to make and engrave photo frames and also rings with a heart inlaid. They used to sell them for money to purchase extra food. They would give me money to buy them loaves of bread. I have seen them go off work of an evening with two 4lb loaves under their great coats. Their guards must of known what was going on but took no notice, as they were a decent lot of chaps when they were working in the Stiperstones area.

From "Recalling the Past" by George Evans

During the 1914-18 War the German prisoners of war were housed in a big shed called the Cabin at The Bog. It was an outstanding building in its day, being one of the biggest buildings around, and the best. The Germans were good craftsmen, even then. The prisoners built the line for the endless rope which stretched fourteen miles, seven miles one way and seven miles the other, bringing coal uphill and taking barytes down to Malehurst. There were between four and five hundred buckets on the fourteen mile rope moving all the time. A steam engine at The Bog used to turn the rope which was one and a half inches in diameter. At any given time there'd be 20 – 30 ton on the rope on each seven mile stretch with 4-5 cwt in each bucket. Each pole was set in concrete, then underneath that again was a massive block of concrete; so you'd got 4 blocks on the top to steady the poles and the massive block underneath to consolidate it. Where they couldn't get the trestles high enough they cut ravines out of the hillside for the buckets to pass through. The buckets were about sixteen feet from the ground or nearly a hundred feet where they passed over the hillsides. It was taken down around 1930. It was only up about fifteen years and was quite a feat of engineering. My granny told us a story that when they were so poor they couldn't afford any coal, and the weather was very bad, one of the Germans would get a stick and tip one of the overhead buckets of coal. They knew how to tip them because they made them. Then granny would have had 4cwt of coal free.

Henry Jones

The German prisoners were stationed at The Bog and they used to march down the road to do their jobs. They built an aerial ropeway from the Bog to Malehurst, below Minsterley in a straight line from the Bog school to the bottom of the bank at Poulton, like Llandudno and Butlins.

We were marched down the road from school to see the first buckets going down and there used to be a gentleman, his name was Jim Williams and there was a big iron aerial place in the field behind the school and we used to watch him going up there and oiling the wheels. He was there most Mondays to oil them wheels.

There was a very steep part above the Stiperstones where it came straight over the hill and many a time a bucket would slip and you would hear 'em coming bang, bang, bang!

Mollie Rowson

Whilst Mollie was at school Bill Francis was in France fighting, and the following extract, taken from his diaries, shows some of the impact the horrors of the battlefield had on impressionable young minds and the bitterness that lingered after.

13 November 1983
.......So called Armistice Sunday when Ministers of religion, politicians and the establishment perpetuate that old lie of the glorious dead of the two World Wars who died for freedom. Balls! If they had seen how the poor buggers died – bodies torn to shreds and still alive, boys 18-19 with legs blown off moaning, "Mother, oh mother", as their blood gushed out – they would think it anything but glorious. I am reminded of a verse by the poetess Katherine Tynan,

There they go marching all in step so gay!
Smooth cheeked and golden, food for shells and guns.
Blithley they go as to a wedding day, the mothers' sons.

And all the freedom those who came back earned was the freedom to live in poverty while the rich manufacturers of weapons of destruction schemed where they could start the next war.

Bill Francis in uniform

They were all right those German prisoners. Where Mr. Doug Challinor had his garage at the Crowsnest that's where the timber was, and my brother used to go there a lot to those German prisoners. That's where they took all the bark off to make the aerial trestles. There were so many iron trestles as well for the dangerous ones. One trestle came over the road just the other side of the pub at the Stiperstones and it passed over the road again at Whinberry Top on the Farm Lane.

There was a gentleman that used to walk down with those prisoners, he was a prisoner but it seems he had been a schoolmaster and he'd been on holiday from Germany when the war started and he wasn't allowed to go back, so therefore he was kept and he walked the road over these prisoners. He'd bring them down in the morning and he had a different uniform to the others and he was outside Central Stores when they had word that the war had finished and I can see him throwing his hat in the air and I'll never forget it. That would be 1918.

Mollie Rowson

I remember the day the Armistice was signed, the Germans made flags with their red hankerchiefs fastened to a stick and were dancing around hugging each other.

From "Recalling the Past" by George Evans

Army detachments were stationed locally and horses ready for army use were based in the old Parish Hall building at Minsterley. This cavernous and corrugated iron structure had previously been used as a timber mill on what is now the site of Minsterley Creamery.

Years ago he used to be in mining, my father did, but before that, the 1914 (war), he used to break all the horses in at Minsterley these half breds. What do you call them, Arabs and something, to break them in for the army.

Johnny Roberts

Walter Yapp (back left) who was injured in the First World War photographed in a military hospital in France.

The Second World War

In due course most of us found ourselves in the uniform of one service or another. Bunny Rippon emigrated to New Zealand and eventually joined the New Zealand forces, only to be killed in Crete. Jack Davies was killed in Normandy and John Downes died in Tunisia. It is very significant that in practically all the battle zones of World War II, including the Japanese Prisoner of War Camps, there was somebody from Snailbeach. Whatever would Monty have done without us?

Johnny Butler

Local lads made good use of the skills they had learnt in their childhood back on the Stiperstones.

The teacher at 'the Beach School', (Stiperstones School), he learnt a lot of 'em to swim in the big pool. A lot of them did learn there, you know. Well there was one lad as was in the army when they were coming over from Dunkirk, if he hadn't learnt to swim, he'd have been drowned.

Elsie Williams

Johnny Butler

The arrival of 'call up' papers meant the beginning of a whole new way of life.

The recruiting office was down where the Granada was (in Shrewsbury). We went in there and had a trade test. We had a choice the Army, the Navy or the R.A.F. I was interested in planes and had worked on a 'drome so I naturally went for the R.A.F. My first posting was to Penarth, then I went to Weston Super Mare to do my square bashing, then to Chivenor in Devon, from there to Mountbatten and onto Davidstow in Cornwall. Afterwards I went to Northcoates and from there to Iceland. The volcano was due to erupt when we were there but it all settled down again. In the winter it never got daylight and in the summer it never got dark.

On V.E. day I was on duty (at Shawbury) waiting for three squadrons to come back. There was 38 – 40 in a squadron and less than half came back, a lot had got shot down. It was the very last day.

Graham France

Les Hordley in uniform of The Gordon Highlanders

I joined the Navy. I got my call up papers in August 1942 and after three months training on H.M.S. Raleigh I was sent to do training on Landing Craft. We went out to Egypt, round the Cape, up to the Red Sea to Alexandria. We were stationed on the Suez Canal. We were on our way to Sicily when we were torpedoed. The landing crafts weighed about thirty ton. They were blown right over our heads. We scrambled out in to lifeboats and got back to Benghazi. I was out there for about eighteen months. We used to get our mail by submarine.

John Francis

I joined up as a regular, they asked what did I do in civilian life, I told them I was a butcher so they said they'd make me a cook and butcher and sent me to the school of cookery in Halton in Buckinghamshire where I got attached to radio units. We were in the Battle of Britain and in 152 Squadron in Dorset, Iceland and the Shetlands, then a couple of years in India. I had signed for seven years on 25th January 1939 and I left Rawalpindi for home on the day I'd done my seven years. I got home the day Eva, my wife, was twenty-one, 15th March 1946.

Bernard Millington

For some local men active service ended abruptly with capture by enemy forces and incarceration in Prisoner of War camps abroad. For their families back home there was an anxious time of waiting and hoping.

I had had a card from Cape Town and some silver leaves. But then we didn't hear anything other than we were told he was missing. We had a small postcard a year and a half later that was censored (Trevor had been taken as a P.O.W. in the Far East) and then it was ages until we had a card from him. I had never given up hope.

Doreen Rowson

I was vaccinated when I went in the Air Force and I had what they call Vaccination Fever. Now, if you'd been vaccinated before you didn't have any trouble, but we were in private billets in Blackpool, waiting to be posted and we had this vaccination and my arm came up like that and it was the same right out through the end of your fingers. I always remember this lady we were in digs with, she said, "What's the matter Roly?". I said, "Look at my arm." She said, "Yes it's vaccination fever in it." So I said, "Is that what it is?" She said, "Yes, does it pain you?" I said, "Pain you, it's terrible!" She said, "Before you go to bed tonight, come to the kitchen and I'll rub it for you." And she rubbed it with olive oil and within two or three days it was alright.

Roly Johnson

When in India I was bitten on the ankle and had to go to a place in the Himalayas, Chitorgarh, 7,500 feet up, which was back to our climate and it healed up there. There was stacks of British blokes up there with boils and things like that which wouldn't heal in the humid heat on the plain.

Bernard Millington

Under the Essential Works Order mining was a reserved occupation, as was farming. Barytes was used in the Chemical Industry and in the manufacture of explosives during the war.

There was three or four of us that went to sign up. After telling the Sergeant Major I was a lead miner he shouted, "What the hell are you doing here? Get off back to your work!".

Heber Rowson

If the Germans had come, oh my Lord!

Those men who had yet to be called up, or who were needed for essential work at home, enlisted in the Home Guard. Resources, however, were scarce and 'make do and mend' was often the order of the day. Life in what has become known as Dad's Army was not without its moments of excitement and even fear. The lighter side of things was never far away, however, and moments of hilarity are recalled with fondness and candour.

When you were eighteen you had to go into Shrewsbury and register. Once they got your name that was it! Before they called you up in the armed forces, then you had to join the Home Guard. I didn't have a uniform. All they gave me was two flags. I didn't know what they were for! I learnt after they were for semaphore. I had to bring these flags home. These meetings were once a week at Minsterley Parish Hall. They used to parade us around there and I remember them taking us up to Snailbeach in the white hillocks there to learn to throw hand grenades. Because I was the youngest they ran out of hand grenades. I was very glad. I was scared to death of these hand grenades. You used to have to throw 'em and they was live hand grenades and they went off with a great big bang and spluttered the stones everywhere. There was a shortage of rifles then and we had no other weapons! Mr Lehmann was the main man.

John Francis

The local Home Guard

An incendiary came down right on the works. Well in the Home Guard they'd been told not to throw water on it. They'd to throw dirt. And of course this thing came down showing our house all up. Edwin, like a silly beggar took off with a bucket of water and they'd told him to take dirt. I was out in the yard in the dark when he put the water on it and it all burst up! I thought oh dear he's surely got it 'cos he was there. As I went running down he was running back. We passed one another by the gate! Oh it was funny – real funny. You can laugh now, but you didn't laugh then, though.
Lydia Harrison

An incendiary bomb dropped in our hedge – number eight. Well, dad was running all over the shop putting cinders on it. Dad had got a good fire – you know a real draw fire. The Home Guard was across the bottom of the Lordshill bank and they'd seen it, so one of the men come and he said, "Mr Hewitt, what do you think you'm doing?" He said, "Well I'm douting this blooming thing!" "Well put earth on it not ashes on it you're making a fire!" Dad was putting cinders on it! That was in our hedge that was.
Peggy Chidley

I'm afraid if it was left to the Home Guard we should have all been dead! Some of them didn't know their right hand from their left. They used to go on the 'sludge pool' (a flat section of the White Hillocks at Snailbeach) as was for training. Uncle Fred Blakemore, he went and our John went. George Williams used to take them. He'd been a soldier and he used to train them. One night he shouted, "Right hand turn", and our Johnny went to the left! They had bits of sticks for guns. The women used to go up on the black hillock to watch them training. We did have a laugh. If the Germans had come – Oh my Lord!
Lydia Harrison

We had to carry identity cards, it had your name and address and date of birth on it. My number was OG11 123. I got stopped on the bridge at Plox Green this one morning and asked to see my card. I hadn't got it. I said, "Well you know who I am", it was Bert Webb who had stopped me and he worked at the same shop as me on the van. He said, "You've got to go back for it!." I said, "Don't be silly Bert you know who I am!." He made me go all the way back to Crowsnest for it – I tell you what when I got to work I gave him Bert!

Susie Hartshorn

War generated a need for vigilance up on the Stiperstones as much as anywhere. Rotas were formed so that each night a watch was kept as German bombers passed overhead on their way to and from the cities of northern England.

Crowsnest people and Snailbeach people got together and two ladies used to walk every night two at a time from Crowsnest to Snailbeach keeping watch. We'd start at about eleven up till one or two until it went quiet with the planes. That was the 1940s.

Mollie Rowson

As well as fear and danger, war can bring with it the benefits of a buoyant economy and near full employment.

I worked all through the war. At the commencement of the war I was at the Creamery on nights for 3 1/2 d per hour. I got a rise of a farthing per hour! It was seven at night until seven in the morning and then biking home after that. Then we were transferred to the factory making stew for the soldiers. That was hard work and cold – oooh the meat would be frozen. Then I got a job at the shop in Minsterley and I was there all through the rest of the war.

Mollie Rowson

We saw a lot and we heard a lot

The message would go through to Malehurst [barytes mill] that an air-raid was imminent. Wallace Evans would then have to ring Minsterley Creameries where I was on the switchboard. I had to notify whoever was in charge of the siren to set it off. When the air-raid was over another message would come through to sound the 'all clear'.

Verna Lewis

The first thing we knew about war was nearly twelve months after. I think it was the August about nine o'clock. My brother was working at Malehurst then and Mum and Don and I were at home and all of a sudden we heard the screeching.

Mum and Don had gone to bed and the dog was outside and I heard this screeching. They dropped a bomb just below Central Stores in Mr David Oldfield's field. Oh it was a noise! The table jumped, the doors jumped, the dog howled outside, I got the dog in. We slept under the table and many nights we had under the table.

Mollie Rowson

The bomb went off in that field below and the lamp went up 'whoosh', like that and out he went. We were sitting there playing cards.

Gordon Cook

As we were coming up past the Farm Cottages – well, my goodness, we fell to the ground! There was this terrific explosion and there was a plane hovering around and he dropped this high explosive down below Davies'. It sent us to the floor and Mr Yapp lived in one of the cottages down there and he come home with us 'cos we were so frightened.

Elsie Rowson

One night a rain of incendiary and explosive bombs were dropped. They missed their target, but gave local people a host of vivid memories which have lingered long.

The German aeroplanes used to come straight over Peggy's Hill right above where we lived – droning, and there was incendiary bombs dropped once and all our hills were on fire right from Snailbeach to the Grit Marsh and the following day it was given out from Germany that they'd hit the ammunition dump that went from Bishops Castle down to Plowden. It never had, but our hills were all on fire. There was a big hole at The Bog just by the side of the school where a big bomb had fallen. Our hills were not fit to walk on for a long long time after that and I wonder now sometimes are they alright!

Mollie Rowson

Quite a lot of bombs dropped on the hill in 1943. The Germans thought they were bombing an ammunition dump. Two hundred and fifty explosives and five to six hundred incendiaries. There was fires all over the place. We ploughed an incendiary bomb up – unexploded sixteen to eighteen years ago (early 1980s) the fin and all was intact!

Henry Jones

Our hills were all on fire

"……… and then of course the incendiaries and the high explosives that dropped all around and dad listened to Lord Haw Haw [William Joyce broadcasting pro German propaganda on the radio] *the next night and he said they burned all the ammunition dumps out, but they'd missed 'em 'cos they were down under Pontesford Hill. The bus was coming up the Farm Lane by the church, and this flare was hanging in the sky. Oh it lit the whole place up and they started there, the incendiaries. The only house to get hit was a little house up the Shop Lane. That was the only empty house there was in the village. It had got a tin roof on, and it went straight through the roof.*

Elsie Rowson

William Joyce, Lord Haw Haw, broadcasted, "The British people are sitting by empty grates!" And we had a fire roaring up the chimney at The Green. My dad shouted, "Liar!"

Wallace Evans

You had a wireless if you were lucky. It ran off accumulators that were filled with acid and distilled water which had to be charged to get the wireless to work. Tom Parry, Central Stores, had a generator that charged the batteries. We were fortunate to have a wireless – when it went – if the accumulators ran down you didn't get any news.

Graham France

When the weekend come, we went round on bikes and we found out where they dropped these incendiary bombs and some of them dropped on the Marshes in the soft ground and they never went off, they had to strike a hard surface to go off. I can remember carrying them about, live ones, trying to set them off. I didn't know the danger of them then. I remember trying to set them off by swinging them over on the hillocks.

John Francis

We'd been to a dance at The Bog and we started to walk home and from Bergam Corner you could see Liverpool all lit up. The'd bombed a big place at Liverpool and the sky was all red.

Mollie Rowson

I went to a little dance at Snailbeach in the hall and that night Aston Hill, here, was all ablaze, and I never stopped to change my shoes, in those days you took your dancing shoes, I ran home to my mum and Don, all the way to Crowsnest in my dancing shoes. I don't know what became of the others I was too terrified for words it was terrible!

Mollie Rowson

London people huddled underground in tube stations each night as the bombs fell overhead; Stiperstones folk had alternative places of refuge.

There used to be a very dry level in the Crowsnest up to what we call Parry's Pit on the corner and people from the Crowsnest always went up that level and we used to shelter up there. There'd be a lot of people up that level. Mrs Blakemore from Crowsnest always carried her box, her little tin hat box and she always used to sit on it. I'm sure her money was in it.

Mollie Rowson

The night the hill was bombed I can remember mum carrying a case. "Mum, what have you got in that case?", I said. "It's our policies and bank books, if the house gets bombed I've got them!"

Ruth Chesters

I can recall going up the level at Crowsnest taking shelter. Some of the older people had got their deeds in tin boxes and would bring a paraffin lamp.

Derek Rowson

Fred Blakemore had an old level down by his garden in his field where the bus came down (refers to the accident at

Crowsnest in 1997) *all the Nest people used to go up there. I used to walk from the counting house with our lot all the way over there and I think our Thelma wasn't very old then – she was in the pram. There was nowhere else to go except that old level.*

Lydia Harrison

I was coming off nights about eleven o'clock, up a walking road up ladders and the place was all lit up when I got to the surface and I thought what the hell is going on. I had a motor bike at Huglith and I was home in about ten minutes. On Bergam corner it was just one mass of flame, all Shelve Hill, all Stiperstones and all the Devil's Chair. Bombs were going off everywhere. There was our folks and the neighbour in the house as unconcerned! I said, "You beggars ought to get from here!", I said, " You wants to go outside and have a look at it!" Well they had the shock of their lives. "Well where are we to go?". "Anywhere out of here, if a bomb drops on here we shall be no more!" We went down onto Bergam corner like daft fools. There was a powder house there full of gun powder! We sat on these owd railings there and you could hear the bombs. And our dad said, "Well we've got some sense!" and I said, "Why dad?" " The powder house is there!" Well we didn't know what to do – we thought about it. There's an old level down in Buxton we'll go and get up that, they'll never get us there. Well when we got down there, well the level was full of folks!

There was craters up on the hill you could drive a horse and cart in from these owd bombs!

Heber Rowson

Corndon was a mass of lights we could hear the planes. We went outside and decided we'd better get old Jack Waters from the cottage and there was a lady whose husband was away. So my sister and dad got Jack Waters and my brother and my other sister fetched Mrs Johnson to go in that level at The Bog. Suddenly a bomb dropped by the school we thought the school had had it. We all got up the level and found everybody else was there. It was a rare old night that was.

Les Hotchkiss

Sometimes the 'enemy' came too close for any sort of comfort – and immediate evasive action was called for!

I was working at the Maltings in Ditherington, Shrewsbury. It was all army work then. It was known as 'Rat Hotel'! Men were trained there and it was the very first iron framed building. I used to bike to work through Edge and Nox. I heard a sound like a motorbike – a German aircraft came over very low. I could see the Nazi markings on it, a Swastika on the side – I could almost see the pilot actually. So being by myself I tucked under a tree to be on the safe side. I don't know whether they saw me but I saw them! When the papers came out in the evening they had machine gunned a train at Yockleton Station. I don't think anyone was killed. I heard after they shot the plane down that did it.

John Francis

Poppies on the old mining works at Snailbeach

• 118 •

Anxious to support the 'boys out there' in whatever way they could, the people of the villages and hamlets on the Stiperstones got together to raise funds so that gifts could be sent to men in the forces. They called on their reserves of ingenuity and talent to entertain each other in a variety of successful social events, still remembered today.

All during the war we had plays to get money for our soldiers. We had one play there it was called 'Neighbours of Sunshine Alley', and there was thirty-two boys and girls in it, in their teens. We travelled all around giving that play, Hope, Westbury, Pontesbury, Minsterley Show night. I never was in the play. I was getting all their clothes and dressing them up and seeing they did the thing right and all that type of thing. And we sent all our local boys four pounds sixteen shillings one Christmas and my sister had some wonderful letters that she received back from some of those lads. Wonderful letters they were so pleased.

We had two concert parties, one with the little ones. I've seen people at the Village Hall standing on boxes looking in through the windows at those children. It was a wonderful time. We worked so hard.

When the war finished one of the little boys who was in that play, he was only a boy then in the play, came and asked me to start again. I said there's nothing to go for now!

Mollie Rowson

On 15th February 1944 the spectre of death cast its shadow on the local area. A Whitley bomber Mk 5 number BD420 of Operational Training Unit, Tilstock, Shropshire was flying over the Stiperstones range when it lost height, crashing into Mytton Dingle at 18.00 hours, killing all five crew members. It had been towing a Horsa glider which had a carrying capacity of twenty-seven soldiers and two pilots. The glider made a safe landing in the Hope Valley.

The five crew members of the Whitley bomber were:

Flight Sergeant R R Brown	pilot
Warrant Officer E A Creber	navigator
Sergeant R F Hodges	air bomber
Sergeant J T Brownhill	wireless operator / air gunner
Sergeant H Little	air gunner

We were sitting having our tea and heard it. I ran and Jim Harper ran. We ran all the way up Mytton Dingle. When we got there it was an inferno. I shall never forget this lad lying there, he'd been thrown clear but his back was broken and his neck. There was just a flicker of life there. Every lace in his boot was split as was his belt. It was a Whitley bomber. The scar was on the hill for years and years. I went up sometime later and found a half crown and an old penny and a ha'penny. I've got them in an old tin and I'd never spend them.

Wallace Evans

I went to school one morning and all the kids were sitting on the wall and I said "What are you looking at?" and they said a plane had crashed in Mytton Dingle I looked up there and one of its wings had gone round about the Red Ball. It had come over from The Long Mynd side and as he flew over Mytton Dingle he lost height and crashed into the rock about 60 to 70 yards below the summit. Everything disintegrated and a lot of it rolled down into the bottom, all in pieces and exploded. I think there was five people killed in it. Of course there was a lot of activity that day ambulance and police all day. They lugged it away on low-loaders, parts of the fuselage and bits of wings. They was days and days getting it down and lugging it away, I was about eight or nine.

Henry Jones

Oh yes, we all went up there (to the plane crash). *There were eight men I think and one on 'em was alive and one woman run down to the bottom of the hill to get water but by the time she got back he was dead.* Elsie Rowson

Connie Read was one of the young women whose service during the War involved agricultural work as a 'Landgirl'. Billetted on farms throughout the country, they worked long hard hours for their keep.

In the morning on one farm we had a cup of tea, then milked. Then we had a boiled duck egg on dry bread an inch thick and scrapings of a jam jar. They had our ration books but we never saw butter. Midday you would have some more inch thick bread with jam scraped on and off again. I was so piping hungry that I used to eat the top half of another man's sandwich because he couldn't open his mouth wide enough to bite it, so he used to take the top off and I'd eat it! And then dinner would be potatoes, an oxo cube thrown in and a heap of boiled swede – no meat – then some rice pudding made with skim. So you went out feeling like a barrage balloon and within ten minutes you could bite your finger nail ends with hunger.

More dry bread with jam scraped on and off in the middle of the afternoon. Then after your twelve hour day at seven o'clock you came in and you had what looked like toasted cheese. It went in as a piece of cheese the size of your thumb in the middle of an enamel plate in a pool of skim milk and it went in the oven and it smelled lovely and it tasted quite nice but you had to eat it with a teaspoon because it was so runny. That was your evening meal and then you had a cup of tea before you went to bed. So most of the time you were absolutely famished. I didn't stay there very long.

Connie Read

Young children, some with their mothers, came to this area from the cities of Manchester, Liverpool and Birmingham to avoid the ravages of war. It must have been a strange world to these city children, some as young as three years of age, many of whom had never seen a farm animal or an expanse of green fields. It would seem a long time in these children's lives before they were reunited with their natural families. It is only in recent years that we can begin to understand how this prolonged separation must have affected some of them.

We had an evacuee, Marcia Addy. She was a child of a cousin of David Oldfield's from Manchester. She was only three. We had her all through the war. She went to the Stiperstones school and she's never lost touch with us.

Ruth Chesters

I was three and a half when I came to stay in Snailbeach directly after the 1940 Christmas blitz on Manchester. My grandmother was from Snailbeach and it was to her nephew, David Oldfield, that I first came, moving after a while to stay with my great auntie Annie Oldfield at 2 Windsor Cottage. When Auntie Annie became too ill to manage I went to live with 'Auntie' Esmer, 'Uncle' Bert and their daughter Ruth Davies at 23 Snailbeach where I was

spoilt rotten. It must have been a great worry to them as I played in dangerous places around the mine site when I was old enough to play with friends from school. I can still hear Ruth calling me across the works.

"I was as fat as butter and as brown as a nut with wellies and a frock" - Marcia Addy pictured on the right

I had an interesting childhood, I can remember running up the spar hills, playing on the old engine outside the shed, having a playhouse complete with fireplace below the mine office, finding and eating wild strawberries in the Compressor House as I waited my turn to jump from one big block to the other, sliding down the metal bars which formed a slide by the mine shaft, going through the tunnel under the mine, having my swing in the Rowan tree, making mud pies and decorating them with flowers.

My friend the pig, how he enjoyed having his back scratched and sad though I was at his demise, how I loved to help rub the salt into the flitches.

I loved going to Sunday School both morning and afternoon, staying to afternoon chapel and often going in the evening too. I learned to read by knowing the hymns off by heart and then following them in the hymn book. My Sunday school prize for May 1943 when I was six was a small copy of 'The Methodist Hymnal'. The presentation label, written by Jim Price, I still have that and really treasure it. I started school able to read. Perhaps not 'the cat sat on the mat' but I could read words like Salvation and Redemption!

I can remember wetting myself at the Sunday school anniversary. I had my new dress on and a new straw bonnet. Mum and dad came quite often but travel was restricted during the war. They came for holidays and stayed. I never made much fuss when they went, but having known four homes by the time I was four years old my time at Auntie Esmer's was the most settled and secure I had known. I was as fat as butter and brown as a nut with wellies and a frock.

I don't mean to be flippant, and have the greatest sympathy for people whose lives were shattered by the war but

This letter was sent during my stay in Snailbeach. I did not ask to go home but instead asked for my bike and bird (a budgie which died during the blitz) to be sent to me. (Marcia Fletcher)

for me it was wonderful and I value the years I spent in Snailbeach. When I think of the war, I can honestly say, I had a lovely time.
Marcia Fletcher (nee Addy)

I remember a lane and a man walking towards us and this lady saying, "This is your daddy, your new daddy." And I thought that's not my dad!

The last straw had come when our house in Liverpool was bombed. I had years of nightmares of fires and things following the bombing. Siren sounds on old war films can still turn me to jelly. Mum had to send us away to the country after that. She sent my three sisters and me, I was only four. My brother who was only two stayed with my mum in Liverpool.

We never had any family life after that. I saw my sisters every now and again, but we were not encouraged to be together even though we were all within half a mile of each other. I remember starting school and someone saying, "That's your sister." But we were strangers. I was made fun of because of my Liverpool accent; children are cruel.

I never saw my mum again until I was twenty-one. She kept in touch with us. I always had books and lovely clothes because she was a dress maker. She tried to come and see us and got as far as Shrewsbury station but it was impossible to get all the way out here and back in time to catch the train back and she had two young children with her. So she had to go back without seeing us. She was broken hearted. I had seen my dad, he came to see me on a couple of occasions, he was in the army.

When I was twenty-one I went to Liverpool to see her and even though I had never seen her for seventeen years, there had been no photographs, I knew exactly what she looked like.
Gloria Rowson

The war definitely altered everything, it altered farming, farming methods, it altered folk's attitudes to everything, especially their attitude to working on a Sunday, it altered everything.
Jack Pugh

Fourteen local lads made the ultimate sacrifice,
never returning to the Stiperstones.

1914-1918

J Rowson

H.H. Blakeman
T. Adams
W. Bishop
Wilfred Evans
Philip Preece
Oscar Challinor
John Jones
Arthur Betton
Alfred Betton
Eli Pugh

1939-1945

Herbert Davies
Edward Chidley Humphrey
William John Richard Downes

10: Abide with me

In the midst of life we are in death

Death, and in particular early death, was a regular visitor to the communities of the Stiperstones in the early years of the 20th century. The effect of losing a breadwinner to families already living on the poverty line could be devastating. Such tragedies, however, were met with a stoicism born of hardship and self-reliance. Tears were shed but the quiet support of friends and neighbours was always to hand.

Respect for the memory of the deceased, and the family and loved ones who survived them, were the guiding principles behind the many customs and traditions which surrounded country funerals. Whether it was the colour of the bearers' gloves, the food provided at the home, or the carrying of the coffin to its final resting place, great care was always taken to ensure that everything was as it should be and as it always had been. Dignity and care were the watchwords, as whole communities joined as one, both to organise the funeral and to grieve together at the loss of 'one of their own'.

Funerals were ceremonial occasions and well attended by the local people. Sarah Ann Evans' first experience of a funeral left a vivid memory.

The first funeral I ever saw was from the Roundhill, and it was Mrs. Hamer, and I remember me and my cousin looking down on them from the hill. All these men used to come as bearers. The family always supplied the bearers with black ties and black gloves. First of all they would have a service outside the house. Then they would go around with wine, sponge-finger biscuits and a piece of fruitcake. They would then set out to walk, carrying the coffin, there was no hearse or anything like that. They would walk across the fields to Hope, Shelve or even Wentnor. The men would walk in front carrying the coffin and the mourners walked behind. Four men in front would drop back and swap with the four that was carrying the coffin.

The whole family would be in mourning for twelve months, even the children would wear black for a full twelve months.

Sarah Ann Evans

Funerals were essentially ceremonial occasions and particularly important was the mode of dress, both at the funeral and thereafter.

It was the noted thing that if anybody died and you was asked to be a bearer, you had black gloves and a black tie, except if it was a someone young, then it was all white, white gloves and a white bow.....

Gordon Cook

I remember when my dad died, we went to Shrewsbury to a Churching Shop and you told them you wanted clothes for mourning and if you didn't have black you had grey.

Ruth Chesters

Dad was a bearer at the funeral of Mr. Hutton of Minsterley Hall. Dad had a high silk hat. You don't have to finger mark one of them! It came in a case with gloves as well. Us kids got this high silk hat and put it on and paraded around in it. Dad played hell with us for that.

Della Pugh

A terrific lot of women had veils after the First World War and were somberly dressed. I can remember my granny, she was quite old. Her probably wasn't really that old she might have been sixty or seventy. She always wore a black veil but she had lost her husband. You had to give her a kiss through this veil, she'd give you a tanner and you'd think 'here goes' and then you had to kiss her through this veil.

Jack Pugh

Floral tributes also played an important role in the ceremony.

All I can remember is funerals. It was always funerals in them days. I couldna bear chrysanthemums, there was always big wreaths of 'em at funerals. They had loads of flowers at funerals in them days. Tom Pinches

Death could strike at any time, of course, sometimes without warning and sometimes after long periods of pain and suffering.

IN LOVING MEMORY

OF

NANCY,

THE BELOVED DAUGHTER OF SAMUEL AND ELIZABETH RIDGE, OF SNAILBEACH.

WHO DIED NOVEMBER 4TH, 1911.

AGED 6 YEARS.

Interred in Snailbeach Primitive Methodist Chapel Yard, November 8th, 1911.

IN LOVING MEMORY

OF

IRIS,

THE BELOVED DAUGHTER OF SAMUEL AND ELIZABETH RIDGE, OF SNAILBEACH.

WHO DIED SEPTEMBER 26TH, 1912.

AGED 18 MONTHS.

Interred in Snailbeach Primitive Methodist Chapel Yard, September 30th, 1912.

'Jesus called a little child' – Two little sisters (pictured above), cause of death unknown, a common place occurrence in those days.

I remember a little girl called Naomi, she played with me at the farm, out on the green. At dinner time she went home and got some matches and set her little white pinafore on fire. She was burnt to death. She was only five or six and was buried at Snailbeach Chapel.

Della Pugh

My dad was a miner and he died at forty-seven from silicosis. I was thirteen when he died and I remember having to take the money round to Fred Jones straight away. It was £8 for a funeral then.

Tom Pinches

For the people of the Stiperstones, the Snailbeach Mining Disaster in 1895 is an event which will probably never completely fade from the communal memory.

The weather during the first quarter of the year 1895 was of exceptional severity. Snow, sleet, gales and frost, the like of which had rarely been experienced before in the district, prevailed week after week. The snow drifted wherever there was shelter or support for it. Severe frost hardened it, while more snow fell from time to time. Work had temporarily ceased at the Snailbeach lead mine due to severe weather.

It was in such weather conditions as these that the miners, some travelling several miles, made their way through the darkness to the mine in time for the 6.00am shift on the morning of 6th March. That morning George Williams, the engineman, raised steam and ran the cages three times through the shaft as a test. The winding system consisted of two separate cages, each of which had its own rope passing over pulleys on the headgear to the same drum. The ropes were wound on the drum so as to bring one cage to the surface at the same time as the other cage was at the shaft bottom. In the cage there was room for seven men.

On the third drop the rope broke when the cage was about half way down the 252 yard shaft, allowing it to crash to the bottom, killing all seven miners. Apparently, it was the practice of the engineman, when the cages were not in use, to keep them about half way down the shaft. This meant that the same part of the rope was always on the pulley and it was at this point that it broke.

Members of the day shift waiting at the shaft bottom were horrified at the sight they beheld. The cage, seven foot six inches tall, was reduced to a mere eighteen inches, and yet, when the rescue party descended the ladders to recover the mutilated bodies, it is said that a watch worn by one of the dead was still ticking.

George's Shaft 1872, where the seven miners met their death

The Wellington Journal of 1895 includes a report by W Holyoake, a Snailbeach miner, given at the inquest:-

I went with seven others down the mine in the second cage. There was no jerk in going down. When we got down we lighted our candles and waited till the next party should come down. In two or three minutes we heard the cage coming down. The noise was like thunder. The cage crashed down with the bodies in it. The cage was smashed up. The rope came down on top of the cage. We signalled up at once and proceeded to take the rope away by drawing it along the level. The rope was knocked about. We had to knock the cage to pieces to get the bodies out. There was no sign of life in any of them. I had every confidence in the rope and it always looked perfectly safe.

The verdict was, accidental death caused by the breakage of a defective rope, and the jury thought that the rope had not been properly looked after and had been used too long. Although the Mines Inspector felt that the company and their agents should be censured, there was no breach of the Metalliferous Mines Regulations Act as it stood at that time.

Mining has always been a dangerous occupation, but more so before the introduction of Health and Safety legislation. It was common to economise wherever possible by using machinery and haulage ropes for far longer than would be allowed today. In some mines, maintenance merely consisted of an occasional visual check. This would be unlikely to identify worn winding ropes about to break. There were many instances of ropes breaking with fatal consequences and this is what happened at Snailbeach mine in 1895.

In all such disasters it always seems to happen that, by a stroke of luck, someone escapes at the expense of another. It was so in this case. George Lewis' son, Will, was due to enter this cage, but on his father remarking that they had forgotten their drills, (which had been brought up the previous day to the blacksmith's shop for sharpening) the young man ran back to the Miners' Dry (the building in which the miners changed before and after their shifts) to get them. When he stepped out, Arthur Wardman took his place. The signal was given and the cage moved downwards to its destruction. Will Lewis came out of the Miners' Dry just in time to see the broken end of the steel rope flying overhead back to the engine house, where George Williams, the engine driver, had a narrow escape from its recoil.

Rumours were flying around on the day of the accident about how many and which men had died. It was said that all the men who went down that morning had been killed. Mrs Anne Blower was told that her husband had died. She had a stroke and died the next day. Her husband however, had not been killed at all.

My grandfather had forgotten his lunch the day of the mining disaster and had turned back home for it, otherwise...........
Mary Challinor

My grandmother had three sons, she was expecting a child and the shock of hearing about the accident caused her to have a miscarriage and it was a little girl.
Emily Griffiths

The victims were Andrew Dorricott (50) Snailbeach, Joseph Evans (45) Perkins Beach, George Lewis (46) Pennerley, Richard Oakley (60) Minsterley, Thomas Jones (32) Stiperstones, John Purslow (52) Wagbeach and Arthur Wardman (27) Gorsty Bank.

In Loving Memory of
THE LAMENTABLE DEATHS OF
JOSEPH EVANS, GEORGE LEWIS, ARTHUR WARDMAN,
Age 45.   Age 45.   Age 27.
THOMAS JONES, RICHARD OAKLEY,
Age 37.   Age 60.
ANDREW DARRICOTT, AND THOMAS PURSLOW,
Age 50.   Age 52.
Who were killed at Snailbeach Lead Mines, near Shrewsbury, on Wednesday, March 6th, 1895.

Little they thought their time so short,
In this world to remain,
As from their homes they went away,
And they thought to return again.

The families of these men were never to receive a penny in compensation. Reverend Cope, the Methodist Minister, visited the bereaved families after the disaster and his, *assurances that the exit of the departed was a glorious change*, apparently gave much comfort.

Only Arthur Wardman is buried at Snailbeach. His grave is at Lordshill Baptist Chapel. Two others were buried at Holy Trinity, Minsterley, whilst four were laid to rest in Hope Churchyard, both Anglican Churches. As Emily Griffiths explains, the local nonconformist chapels were not at that time consecrated for burials.

Grave of Arthur Wardman at Lordshill Chapel

There was definitely some antagonism between the nonconformist churches and the Church of England, and in some cases it was very bitter. A nonconformist minister could perform a burial in a Church of England graveyard, but the incumbent could claim the fee and invariably did. So you might have to pay double if you wanted your own minister at the burial. At one time the only places for burials were Hope Church, Shelve Church or Lordshill. People from the Stiperstones would have to go to Hope to be buried. There were no conveyances or hearses. All the men in the area would go to the funeral to help carry the coffin. It was the custom to carry the corpses shoulder high and they never put the coffin down from the time it was picked up until the time they arrived at the church. To walk

Grave of Richard Oakley at Holy Trinity, Minsterley

from the Stiperstones over the fields was a long trek over very rough country.

It was one very snowy day and the men slipped and slid and fell down, but they never put the coffin down. They got over to Hope but they were a few minutes late.

They got to the lych gate and the Rector wouldn't start to conduct the burial for half an hour. That was the penalty they had to pay for being a few minutes late. Those men had to stand holding the corpse shoulder high for that half hour after carrying it all the way from the Stiperstones!

"To walk from the Stiperstones over the fields was a very long trek."

There were a variety of services which had to be carried out following a death and of necessity they had to be carried out quickly and therefore locally.

There was a Mrs. Fountain that lived at The Bog. She had a son called Ivor, he was about twelve years old. They came staggering to the back door of the pub one night. She was leaning on him, poor kid! It wasn't long before she popped her clogs......then she was put on the dining room table. They had the post mortem in the garage. I remember that they put the bar room tables out there so they could stretch her out. They absolutely reeked of disinfectant for weeks because we had them back in the pub after!

Walton Humphrey

Dad paid £10 for me to have an apprenticeship with a carpenter. As an apprentice carpenter I had all sorts of jobs, one of which was making coffins. We'd get an order for a coffin and go to BMSS [builders' merchant] to get the oak slabs. The oak was wet, not seasoned, and we oiled it with linseed oil. Me and Bill Davies, who was training me, we'd make a coffin in a day.

John Francis

Emily Griffiths recalled an occasion when the coffin proved to be of use in a slightly unusual way.

There was an old couple who lived at Pennerley and the old man had always promised his wife two things if she predeceased him; she would always be carried shoulder high over the Roundhill to Shelve Church to be buried, and that he would always keep her false teeth! The day of her funeral was terrible weather, snowdrifts yards high over the Roundhill, and the local butcher offered to take his horse and cart and convey the corpse round the road to Shelve. Being a sensible old man he agreed for this to happen. Then when he opened the cupboard door, he saw her false teeth there grinning at him, he thought the best place for them was in the coffin with her!

Emily Griffiths

Grave digging has never been an easy task, and for Glyn Price carrying out the job was not without incident.

I went all over the place digging graves for Tom Jones, all over the district as far as Ditton Priors.

I dug a grave up the Methodists in Snailbeach and I happened to go up just before the funeral – I thought I'd better check the grave. When I got there I had the biggest shock of my life, at the lowest corner water was running out, the grave was full and overflowing and that was two hours before the funeral.

I bucketed it all out – I had to keep dipping buckets in, and while they were in church I was down in there bucketing out until Tom gave me the wire that they was coming out, and then I had to jump out and go and hide behind a tree.

Another, at Norbury, by the time they'd gone out of the cemetery and I could fill in the grave, the coffin was level with the top of the soil. It was floating on the water.

At Ditton Priors it was all in sand, and when I got there just before the funeral it was all cracks, the earth had cracked all around the grave. I put as many planks as I could get across and around. Just as they got out of the cemetery I heard this whoosh and the whole lot had collapsed in, each side and the end had all gone in and left me a pool hollow.

I've dug graves at Shelve, that's in rock, rock all the way down as soon as you get the surface off. Hanwood was stony almost like beach pebbles. Westbury was stony as well. Tom could have as many as three funerals a week, he was very concientious and used to worry about it. His dad did it before him and he used to make his own coffins.

Glyn Price

"In the midst of life we are in death"

A poem written by the Rev. John Cope and dedicated to the three lay preachers, Andrew Dorricott, Joseph Evans and George Lewis killed in the Mining Disaster of 1895.

Both Andrew, George and Joseph are to Pilgrim City gone,
With faces bright and robes most white, they are shining like the sun;
Their arduous toil is o'er, and they lean upon the breast,
Of Him who died to lead them to Canaan and to rest.

We preachers shall surely miss them, both their voices and their smiles;
But heaven has grown the richer since they joined the undefiled;
They've gone through the valley of darkness, the rolling river is passed,
They've reached the grand old country, after time's long wintry blast.

Our brethren have gone before us, they see the King's bright face,
They dwell with Him in glory, and magnify His grace,
Just now we'll go and join them in that fair and happy place,
And we'll sing the same old story of Christ's redeeming grace.

Appendix I

A brief history of the South West Shropshire Metal Mines

The Shropshire ores are generally held to come from hot liquids rising from deep in the earth, which found their way into fissures in the rock. Lead ore (galena) and zinc (spalerite) were formed first, followed by calcite, then baryte. Quartz is probably a late addition as it is found coating all the other minerals. Other minerals associated with the district and found in small quantities are witherite and fluorite.

The history of lead mining in Shropshire dates back to at least Roman times. Roman workings were probably shallow, confined to open-cast work on the outcrops, although some mining was probably carried out in small shafts and adits (horizontal tunnels). Evidence of Roman mining activity discovered in the Stiperstones area includes 'pigs' of lead (a pig of lead is a mass of lead cast into a particular shape), tools, pottery and coins.

Mining methods changed very little in the centuries after the Romans. In 1228, three wagon-loads of lead were sent from Shelve to Builth Castle, indicating that there was an active medieval mining industry. As ore became exhausted, however, the miners had to go deeper, and faced the problem of removing water from the workings. Where adits could not solve this problem, the water was removed manually in barrels drawn up the shaft by windlass or horse whim (winding mechanisms). This continued until the late 18th century when the invention of the steam engine revolutionised the mining industry in Britain.

In 1775, Boulton and Watt formed their famous partnership and began to manufacture steam engines at their Soho Works in Birmingham. The mine adventurers of Shropshire were not slow to take advantage of this new means of power and tall engine houses began to rise beside the spoil tips. After 1800, the Boulton and Watt monopoly expired and engines from other manufacturers appeared on the scene. The mining industry began to expand and by 1850 a view of the Stiperstones would have included a dozen engine houses, each with a tall chimney capped with a plume of smoke.

The power from these engines was not only used to pump the lower reaches of the mine free of water, it also carried the miners up and down the shafts and brought the mineral ore to the surface. Underground the task of the miners was to free the mineral from its surrounding rock and tram it to the bottom of the shaft. Holes were drilled into the rock initially by hand, until the introduction of compressed air in 1881. The holes were filled with explosives and fired, thus loosening the mineral. Typically, there would be two experienced miners, a labourer for heavy shovelling, and another responsible for taking the ore to the shaft bottom. There were two types of miners, 'tributers' and 'tutworkers'. 'Tributers' were paid for the weight of ore mined, usually as a percentage of its value. 'Tutworkers' carried out a whole range of jobs in the mine, including driving tunnels, sinking shafts and transporting the ore. Their wages did not depend on the value of ore produced.

Once it reached the surface, the ore passed through a variety of processes on the nearby 'dressing floors'. In places, some of this work was carried out by women and children working in all weathers with very little cover. The ore was first washed and large pieces broken down to a manageable size by hand. It then passed through a 'crusher' where it was fed between two rollers, sieved manually and collected into pieces of similar size. Different types of machinery were then used to separate the ore from the waste rock, but all worked on the same principle – that the ore was more dense and being heavier would therefore sink faster. Reservoirs were built at most of the mines to provide a regular source of water for these and other processes.

The demand for lead was always unpredictable and as a result price levels were volatile. After a period of high demand caused by the French and Napoleonic Wars (1790s – 1815 approx.) output fluctuated, but continued to rise steadily towards the mid 19th century. The 1860s saw a rise in lead prices and, after a spate of heavy capital investment, the district's lead ore output more than doubled between

1865 and 1875. Production reached a peak in the latter half of the 19th century and, at that time, the Snailbeach and Tankerville companies ranked amongst the largest metal mines in Britain. By 1885, however, cheap imports from abroad had caused the price to fall from a high of £20 to only £11 per ton in the space of seven years. This brought disaster to many of the district's smaller mines which could not make a profit and had to close.

The Stiperstones mines were forced to consider other available minerals that might be raised and sold. Barytes mining allowed them a brief respite at the turn of the 20th century. The mineral was crushed and purified at places such as Malehurst Barytes Crushing Mill, between Pontesbury and Minsterley. It was then used as a filler for earthenware, paper, paint and in other products. Barytes was first commercially produced in the district in the late 1860s. This increased until in the years before the First World War it completely replaced lead production locally, and the Shropshire mines were producing a quarter of the national output. Many of the long established mines were joined or replaced by new producers such as Gatten, Huglith and Perkins Beach. The largest of these, Huglith, near the village of Habberley, closed as recently as 1947.

A number of companies were also formed to re-work the larger spoil tips. Such activity continued until the 1950s and '60s. Today, some of the main mine sites are seeing activity of a different sort. Buildings and other remains at the Snailbeach site have been restored and made accessible to the public as, on a smaller scale, have those at The Bog and Tankerville. Growing numbers of visitors are today discovering the industrial heritage of the beautiful Stiperstones hills.

Ladywell Mine 1970

Appendix II

Interviewees and their dates of birth

Wilfred Andrews	b. 1925	Clifford Lewis	b. 1923
George Balmer	b. 1916-2000	Jean Lewis	b. 1937
John Bennett	b. 1946	Ken Lewis	b. 1914
Jim Booth	b. 1928	Verna Lewis	b. 1925
Doug Boulter	b. 1939	Bernard Millington	b. 1920
Margaret Buckley-Atkins	b. 1916	Henry Owen	b. 1918
Johnny Butler	b. 1920	Nora Pinches	b. 1916-1999
Mary Challinor	b. 1926	Tom Pinches	b. 1924
Ruth Chesters	b. 1928	Glyn Price	b. 1936
Peggy Chidley	b. 1917	Margaret Price	b. 1938
Gordon Cook	b. 1920-1999	Della Pugh	b. 1916
Sybil Cook	b. 1924	Jack Pugh	b. 1917-1998
Bill Evans	b. 1922	Connie Read	b. 1920
Clifford Evans	b. 1937	Johnny Roberts	b. 1921
Sarah Ann Evans	b. 1911	Derek Rowson	b. 1934
Wallace Evans	b. 1925	Doreen Rowson	b. 1919
Graham France	b. 1921	Elsie Rowson	b. 1924
Mavis France	b. 1922	Heber Rowson	b. 1921
John Francis	b. 1923	Mollie Rowson	b. 1908
Millie Gough	b. 1924	Nellie Rowson	b. 1914
Emily Griffiths	b. 1917-1999	Ethel Tomlins	b. 1908
Jim Harper	b. 1925	Dorothy Trow	b. 1915
Dolly Harrison	b. 1915	Harry Trow	b. 1911
Lydia Harrison	b. 1907	Elsie Williams	b. 1911
Harold Hartshorn	b. 1920		
Susie Hartshorn	b. 1926		
Doris Hewitt	b. 1916		
Eileen Higley	b. 1911		
Betty Hordley	b. 1933		
Les Hordley	b. 1926		
Les Hotchkiss	b. 1927		
Walton Humphrey	b. 1921-1999		
Roly Johnson	b. 1921		
Barry Jones	b. 1940		
Brenda Jones	b. 1930		
Henry Jones	b. 1930		
Phyllis Jones	b. 1936		

Taped interviews were carried out between July 1998 and July 2000 by:

Peter Francis
Jilly Knill
Jane Price
Steve Southwick
Sue Southwick
Tom Wall
Kim Yapp